MW01631978

(WHEN WE ARE DANCING)
I GET IDEAS

Lyric by DORCAS COCHRAN *Music by* SANDERS

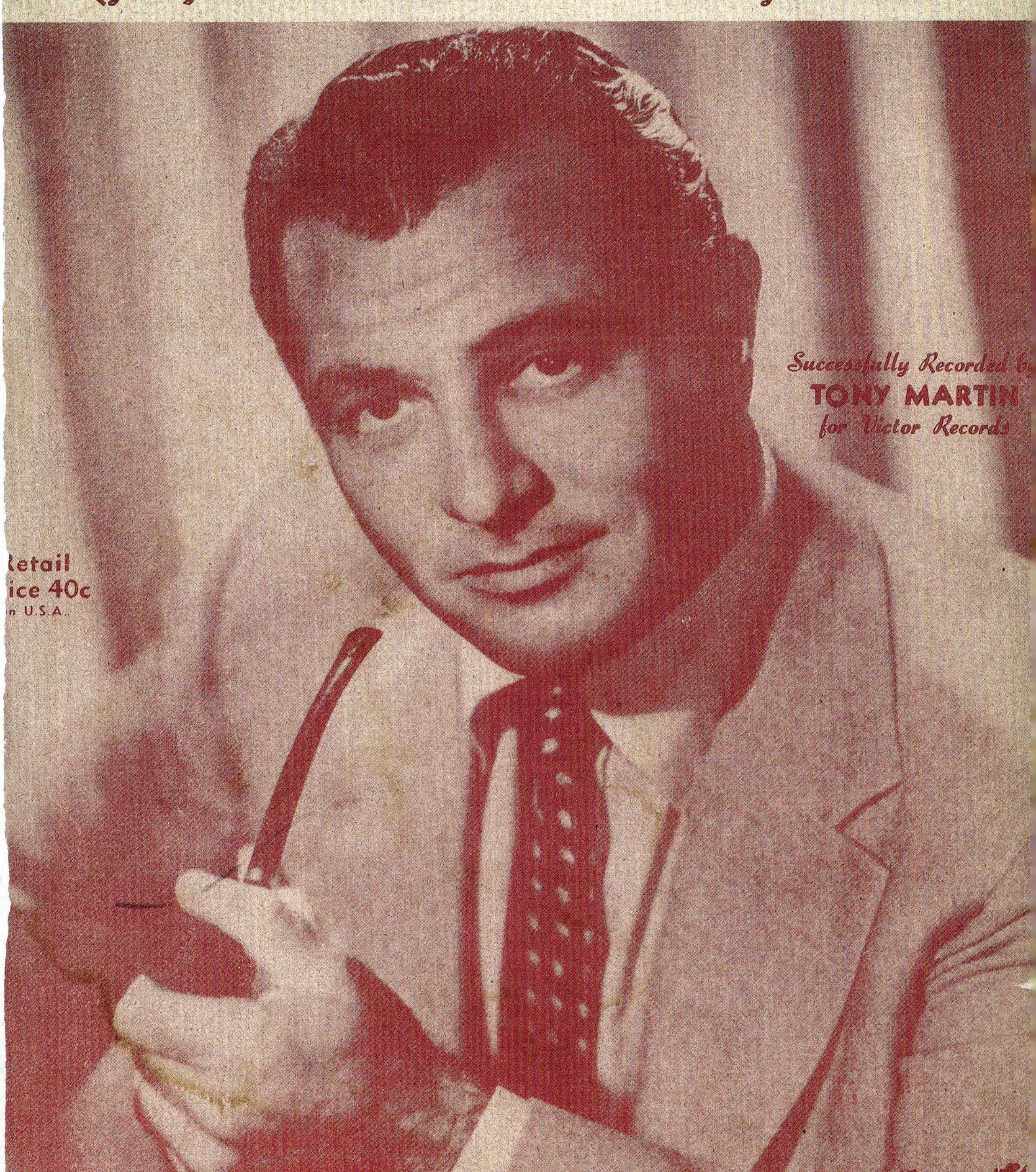

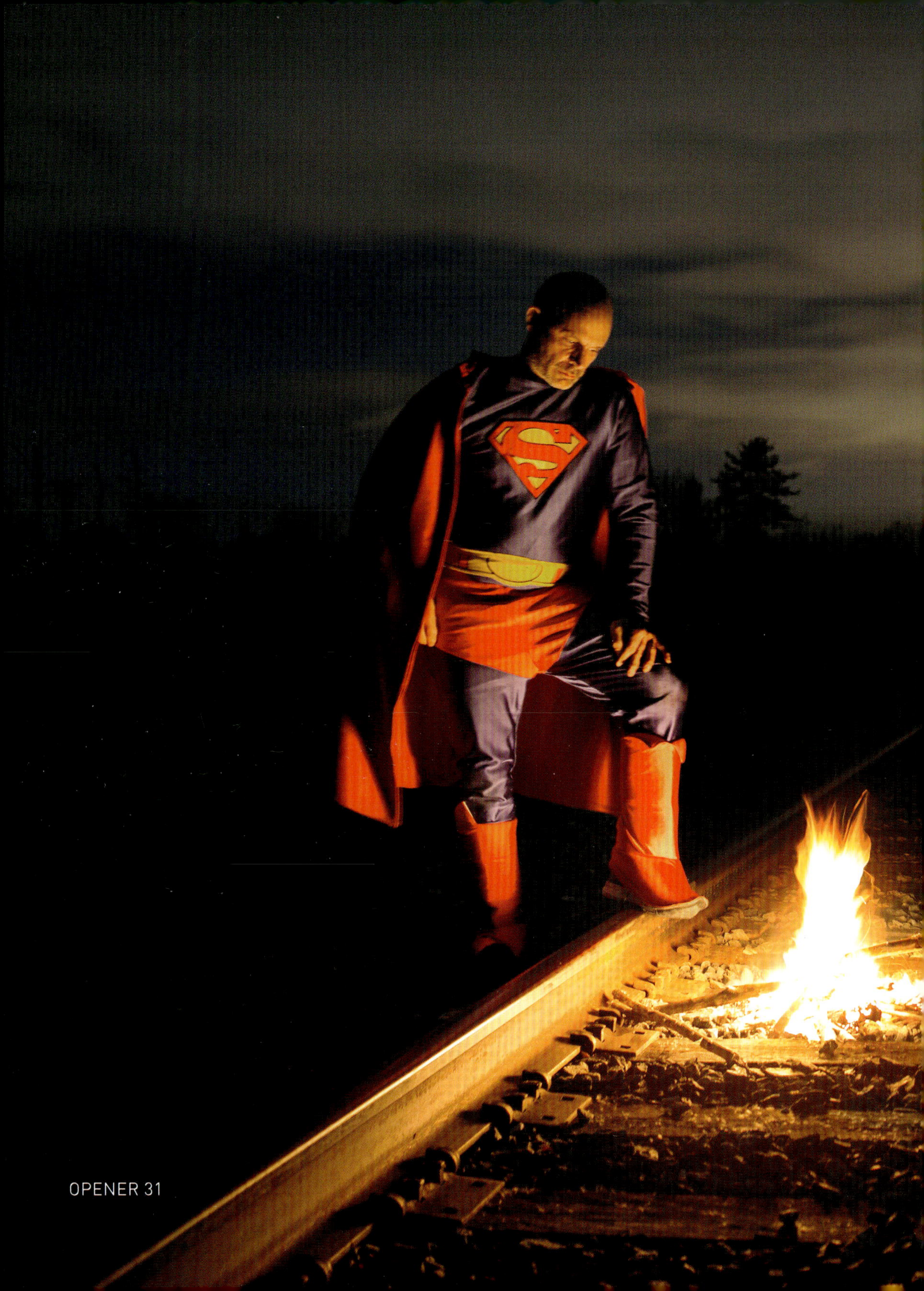

TIM DAVIS

WHEN WE ARE DANCING (I GET IDEAS)

RACHEL SELIGMAN

ESSAYS BY
TIM DAVIS AND
LUC SANTE

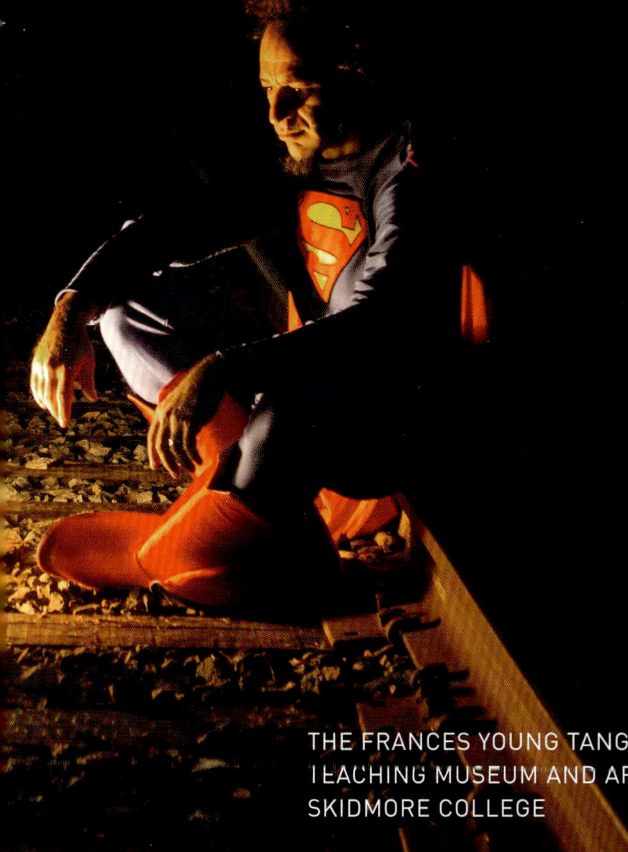

THE FRANCES YOUNG TANG
TEACHING MUSEUM AND ART GALLERY
SKIDMORE COLLEGE

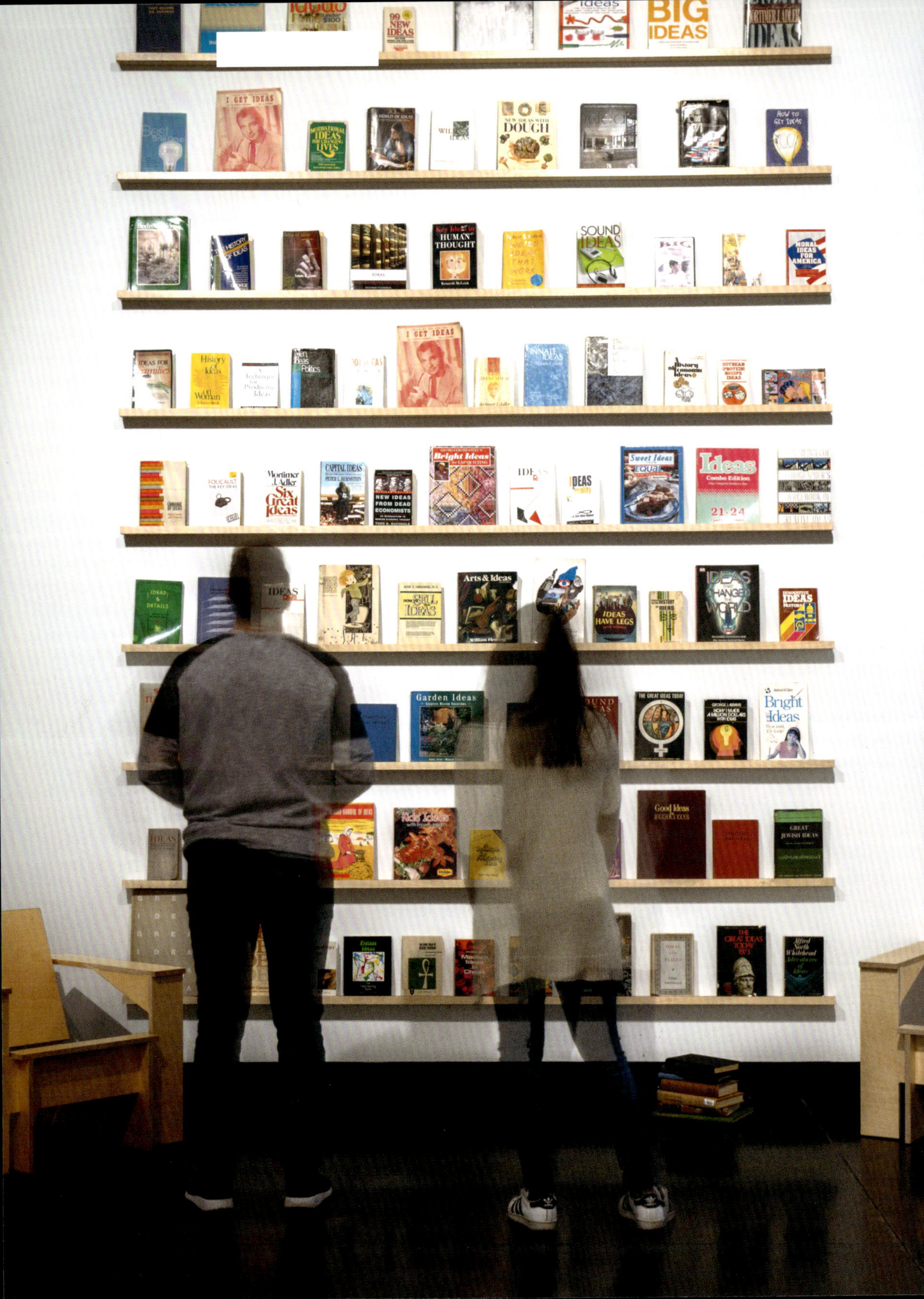

99 NEW IDEAS
BIG IDEAS
MORTIMER J. ADLER
I GET IDEAS
MOTIVATIONAL IDEAS FOR CHANGING LIVES
WORLD OF IDEAS
NEW IDEAS WITH DOUGH
How to Get Ideas
THE HISTORY OF IDEAS
Key Ideas in HUMAN THOUGHT
SOUND IDEAS
MORAL IDEAS FOR AMERICA
IDEAS FOR Families
History of Ideas on Woman
A Technique for Producing Ideas
I GET IDEAS
SOYBEAN (PROTEIN) RECIPE IDEAS
FOUCAULT THE KEY IDEAS
Mortimer J. Adler Six Great Ideas
CAPITAL IDEAS PETER L. BERNSTEIN
NEW IDEAS FROM DEAD ECONOMISTS
Bright Ideas
Sweet Ideas
Ideas Combo Edition
21-24
IDEAS & DETAILS
HOW TO SELL IDEAS
Arts & Ideas
IDEAS HAVE LEGS
IDEAS THAT CHANGED THE WORLD
Garden Ideas
THE GREAT IDEAS TODAY
HOW I MADE A MILLION DOLLARS WITH IDEAS
Bright Ideas
Kids' Ideas
Good Ideas
GREAT JEWISH IDEAS
THE GREAT IDEAS TODAY 1973
Alfred North Whitehead Adventures of Ideas

GOBSTOPPERS EVERYWHERE

A DIALOGUE WITH TIM DAVIS BY RACHEL SELIGMAN

TIM DAVIS IS GOING TO MAKE YOU LAUGH. But don't be fooled: laughter is just the beginning.

His artwork explores the intersection of humor and longing where the abject aligns with the beautiful in unexpected ways. The projects that make up *When We Are Dancing (I Get Ideas)* evoke hope and optimism in the face of terrible odds, desire and longing, pride and pleasure. Davis understands that playfulness can lead us gently toward the complicated truths of what it means to be human. His work is united by an ongoing inquiry into what makes us tick—what we make, and why we create, collect, and share. An artist, writer, and musician, he makes photographs, videos, songs, and sound and sculptural installations. Davis began as a poet, and his visual practice is laced with a love of language. The pleasure of word play is evident in his conceptual process and in his titles.

Rachel Seligman: Where does the title of the show come from?

Tim Davis: It's from a piece of sheet music that I bought in a junk shop called "When We Are Dancing, I Get Ideas." At first, I misunderstood it. I thought it meant that I got my ideas *from* dancing. I didn't realize it was an innuendo. Of course it's as good an explanation as any about where ideas come from. Particularly for me, because my practice is about moving through the world and gathering things that I find. I'm used to anticipating the possibility of finding something interesting to say while moving my feet.

Library of Ideas, 2018
Mixed media
Dimensions variable
Installation view, Tang Museum, Saratoga Springs, New York, 2018

Being a photographer is like being an emperor with no clothes, because at the end of the day, you come back and you don't actually have anything, you don't have any stuff. You just have these collisions of your eyes with the visual world, and your latent images. But accompanying that, for me, has always been a kind of rhizome-like reach for other kinds of collecting. One thing I collect is records. I go into the bins at the junk shops and ask people that I meet if they have any old records in their garages. And in the course of that, I've collected other things. I find that there's a lot of different ways to gather, to glean significance and meaning. The show is a series of these collections arrayed around my main collecting practice, which is photographic.

RS This feels like an optimistic way of being. Have you always been an optimist?

TD I think of myself as eternally optimistic. There's a kind of virginal quality to each day for me. It's like nothing existed before and I feel like I'm starting over, in a good way. But I'm not sure a lot of other people would describe me as an optimist. I mean, just today I was walking around photographing in Schenectady, and I met a guy. I said, "How are you doing?" and he goes, "You know, hanging in there. I can't complain." And I said, "Yes, you can. It's your human right. It's part of our DNA!"

RS I'm interested in the intersection between your optimism and your capacity for the negative. How does that sensibility inform your work? I see a combination of incredible joy, playfulness, and optimism on one hand—and irony, an affinity with the lonely and the abject on the other.

TD I just don't know how to see the world without that kind of complexity. *Complexity* feels like an old-fashioned word in art, like some kind of art school thing: "I'm searching for complexity." But it's like reading James Joyce or Ezra Pound or something. For me, reading those authors was great. I thought, "wow, this doesn't make any sense to me. Interesting! I like it. I'll search further." That feels old fashioned now. We're in a world where we feel like we have to deliver something with clarity. But to me,

It's OK to Hate Yourself, 2015
Video
43 minutes
Installation view, Tang Museum, Saratoga Springs, New York, 2018

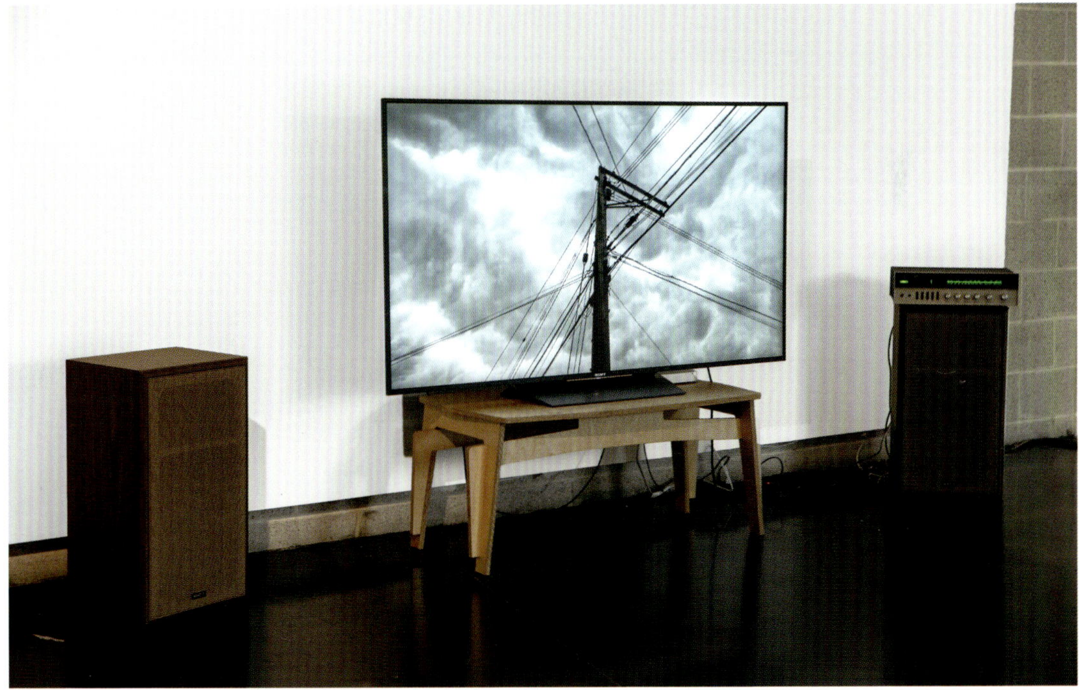

there is no simplicity. Everything either has a weird aftertaste of something else if you linger with it long enough, or, it's like a gobstopper. The world is just a gobstopper! You lick it and it tastes like one thing and then a little while later it tastes like something else.

RS Earlier, you referred to yourself as a photographer. But you're an artist who makes a lot of different things. Do you consider yourself first and foremost a photographer?

TD **Photography is one thing that I'm naturally gifted at. I can express myself to the fullest in photography with hardly any effort. Almost everything else is harder. The reason this show was such a great thrill** was being able to step somewhat outside of what comes naturally and work in ways that are connected to my photographic practice but require a different kind of sense, you know, a different kind of song. These works come out of examining what else I have accumulated along the way and asking myself: why have I accumulated it?

RS What do you see as the relationship between your photography and the rest of these works?

TD The easy thing about photography is taking a picture. The hardest thing is knowing what it all means, where it begins and ends, and what it adds up to. The works in this show were all things that I could see the ends of before I started them. All artists eventually come to a point in a project where they have a vision of the end. Conceptual artists are supposed to be able to see the end before they start. The conceptual artist has the idea, and then they have to make the thing. These were projects where I didn't have to build up a series of blind attempts before knowing the idea. These were things that maybe started as observations at some point, but before I'd ever made any of it, I had the idea and it was basically finite.

In the field, I don't always have the idea framed beforehand, but I've always thought of myself as a conceptualist. I'm out in the world and then I see something, like the reflection of a McDonald's sign off a house window. And I say, "I'm gonna make a picture of that, and if I make a series of those, I've got something." There's an idea there, and it develops from walking around.

RS You started out by saying that you are a collector and that the exhibition is a collection of collections. What does it mean to be a collector?

TD I guess a collector is somebody who has a hunger for significance, has a hunger for divining, and then for digging the well. They just really want to find it. I think finding it is half of the battle. Owning it, or making it into art or figuring out what it all means is another thing. But the hunger to search for it. That's got to be a totally primitive hunting and gathering thing.

I've been thinking about the difference between a collector and a gleaner. Because I feel more like a gleaner, in that for the most part I am taking from somebody else's production. Gleaners go into the fields right after the harvest and they take what's left behind. I'm not making something out of whole cloth usually. I'm not making something that never existed before. That urge to gather something is important to me. And that seems to define everything about my life. It's such a weird and complicated urge.

I think of everything I do as a kind of "groking," which is from *Stranger in a Strange Land*[1]—a pure way of understanding something. Heinlein's Martian word has the literal meaning of "drinking," and to me it means drinking stuff in. And that's what I do all day. I make photographs, and in between the eruptions of pictures, I write songs in my head. And I collect records, I make little art projects, I think about essays. I write about photography while I'm making it. I'm doing all this stuff at once.

RS Music is clearly a huge aspect of your work and of your life. Can you talk a little bit about where that interest comes from?

TD Music is something that I'm not naturally good at. But I think of it as being the religion of my life. It's the thing that I've poured over the details of the most, that I can sit down with other old men and discuss the particularities of, for hours on end. I've never really had a religious practice, but thinking about music, listening to music, collecting music, is close to it. I come from a musical family. My father is a musician and I've been around musicians all my life. I started out making music by writing songs with my little brother. He would make up these crazy songs, like, "I'm the Weirdest Person in the World" and "Big Hair." And then, even though I wasn't trained as a musician, eventually, I started writing my own songs. I'm getting better and better at it. And I now have this band, and we practice a lot. If I had a life coach, they would tell me,

1 Robert A. Heinlein, *Stranger in a Strange Land* (New York: G. P. Putnam's Sons, 1961).

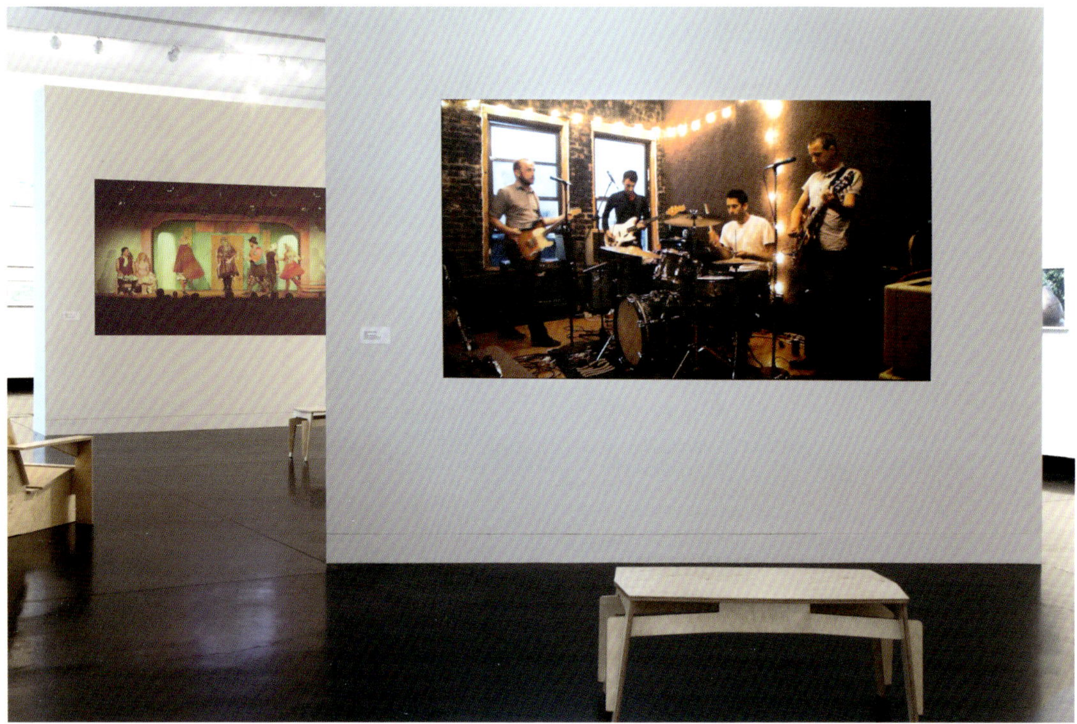

Installation view, *Tim Davis — When We Are Dancing (I Get Ideas)*, Tang Museum, Saratoga Springs, New York, 2018

"Don't waste your time with this." But I am increasingly spending more and more time with music.

Music is a communal thing. And being a photographer is very solitary. Even if you're out in the world, it's just you pressing the button. So it's an interesting, incredibly joyous thing for me to be able to cede control. Music is also this incredibly relevant art form. It's not something that feels specialized and separate from people's lives. It's so intertwined—people are listening to it all the time.

RS How has music entered into your art making?

TD I haven't made any music that isn't contingent upon something visual. I made the album *It's Okay To Hate Yourself*, but I always knew that the real work was going to be the accompanying videos. And the songs I'm writing now are largely written while I'm photographing, and a number of them are about photography. This week, I've been writing a song called "The Acid Casualty's Farfisa." Farfisa is a great vintage Italian organ. Well, I was in this weird junk shop in upstate New York, and there was a Farfisa, and it was just scribbled all over with all kinds of crazy things, and I photographed it. And then I sent the photograph to everybody in my band, and the bassist, John Rosenthal, sent back a text, "It's the acid casualty's Farfisa."

So while I was on this big photo expedition—I drove all the way to Rochester and back from Tivoli via back roads—I was driving along singing, "the acid casualty's Farfisa, is missing almost half its keys-a." So now I've got that, and that's a song. It's now evolved to be a song about things that I've observed in junk shops and antique stores, and the chorus is:

And the salvation army band,
is taking smoke breaks, when they can,
to sit and watch us buy
a little piece of the past,

And so in a way, everything we're describing is a little bit like if you move through the world, you generate friction, like sparks. You generate little sparks as you move through the world and things that you see and observe provide these sparks.

The video *Counting In* was an attempt to show that. They are mostly young people, just living the American dream of starting a band. There's a vicarious thrill in it.

I thought about making a self-portrait at one point, and I thought, "people make self-portraits, what would I do?" I thought about that Dylan record, *Self Portrait.*[2] So, I made a self-portrait that is a bust made up of copies of that record. And you know, luckily, I did it in a time when you could still get them pretty cheap.

RS Aren't you single-handedly responsible for driving up the price of that album?

TD Yeah, I did. It was written about in *Freakonomics*. How one person can affect the marketplace for something.

It's OK to Hate Yourself could have been its own show. I think a lot of people react to that piece much more enthusiastically than they do to

---

2 Bob Dylan, *Self Portrait*, Columbia Records, 1970, Vinyl LP.

everything else in the show. I think it has a really strong emotional content. The songs, in particular, were written at a very unhappy time in my life. So those songs are more personal in a way, and they have a little more pain in them than I'm currently experiencing.

Also, it came at this time where I was shooting video. That happened not because I wanted to make video, but because they made a camera that could also shoot video, and everybody was talking about this camera, and everybody seemed to be getting one. So, I got one. And I actually didn't really like it as a camera at all.

RS For still photographs?

TD Yeah. I didn't like it at all. But the video quality was extraordinary.

A couple of months ago, I was photographing in Rensselaer, which is a magical place. And I encountered one bizarre, beautiful thing after another. I was up around the top of the city in a residential area and I decided to go back down. As I start walking down the hill I hear a car alarm, and I turn around and there's a car completely on fire. The car was just parked on the side of the road, and there was nobody around. And flames are shooting out. But there's a moment in the middle of photographing this where I stop, because I'm making a new video called *Symphony,* about music, which is made up of musical things or sound things that have a visual component, and this thing was making a crazy noise. So, I'm trying to make the best possible picture of it, but I then have to turn the camera off and put it down and shoot video in the middle of it. And it was very hard for me to do. It was like talking in a completely different language in the middle of a sentence. I think I missed the best picture... because I switched.

RS When you were making *It's Okay To Hate Yourself*, you set out to make videos. Were there moments when you thought, "I should be taking a photograph here"?

TD The basic structure of what I do is that gathering, collecting, and gleaning, but I can put different filters on my glasses as to what to look for. That was a year where I didn't really make many photographs, because I didn't like that camera. But I loved the way it shot video. I was at the house in Iowa where Grant Wood painted *American Gothic*. And I had my 4 x 5 camera because I was working on a different project. But I also had that other camera and there was a lawnmower going back and forth in front of *American Gothic*. And I thought, "I've got to take a film of that." That started me thinking about what happens when you make photographs where there's something moving around. And it was really fun, really special. It was like one of those dreams you have where you discover that there is another room in your house or your apartment that you didn't even know was there.

RS You said, in talking about *It's Okay To Hate Yourself*, that a lot of people respond to that differently than some of the other pieces in the show, perhaps more emotionally. How is it that you manage to capture this quality of playfulness, but also poignancy?

TD **I just don't know how to see the world in any other way. And my sense is that if everybody went with me and followed me around, they would feel that way too.**

RS I don't know if that's true.

TD **I wonder. If anyone had walked with me through Rensselaer the other day, and met the immigrant from Senegal who had a six-month-old baby in his arms and kept pigeons. And had seen him take a white pigeon out, and hold it with the baby drooling in the sun... he was so beautiful, and he was so sweet a person but also somebody who doesn't have the easiest life. When you get out into the actual world, beyond statistics and beyond ideology, what you find is that people are complicated and that the world is beautiful and painful, all at the same time. And there just isn't anything else. There are just gobstoppers everywhere.**

RS I know that if we were walking with you, and you stopped and saw that thing, then we would see it too. Because you say to us, look at this and

Installation view, *Tim Davis — When We Are Dancing (I Get Ideas)*, Tang Museum, Saratoga Springs, New York, 2018

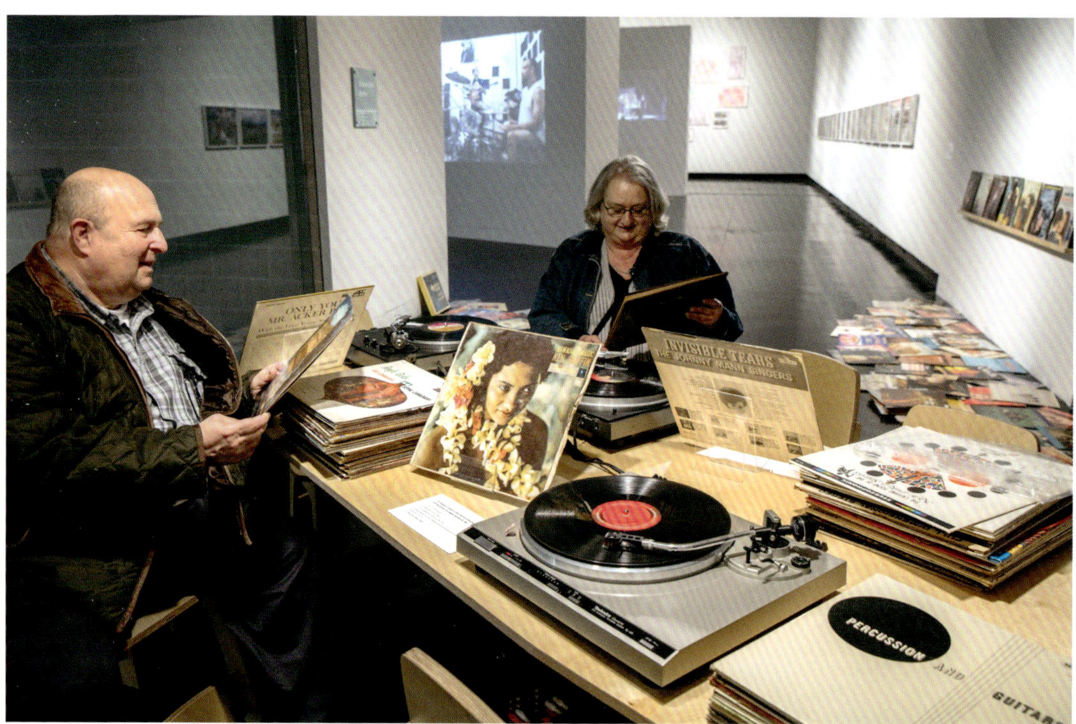

see the essential nature of humanity, which is all of this complexity. But without you as our guide, I worry that we just walk right on by.

TD That's hard for me to understand. When I made the music videos I would meet somebody, and I would put the camera, which looks like a still camera, on the tripod. Then I would say, "I want to take a portrait of you, but I have to go get something out of my car, hold on a second, I forgot something."

And then I would just leave the camera rolling and they didn't know it. And I was gone like five or ten minutes and the person would just kind of stand there and be completely relaxed. That was probably on the verge of being unethical. I could see how somebody would say that it was unethical. On the other hand, these people were all beautiful, amazing, vivid people. And I never made them look bad. I mean, there's a woman who's clearly been beaten up in one of them and that image is in a song that's about heartbreak and the complex beauty of femalehood. Overall, the process that I really believe in as a photographic artist is that we find analogies for our inner world in the outer world. I think it's healthy. It keeps people sane.

RS There is plenty of humor in your work and some of your work is very funny. Why is it that most artists are generally afraid of humor in their work?

TD A fear of not being taken seriously. But do we have to make a distinction between comedies and tragedies in Shakespeare? Not really. The comedies are filled with tragedy and tragedies are filled with comedy. There's no real reason to distinguish. Artists think they have to be taken seriously.

RS Why?

TD I don't know. I think it's stupid. You know how you have friends who are overly serious and ponderous and take themselves too seriously. You don't want to hang out with them, you don't want to invite them over to dinner.

RS They're not the life of the party.

TD I'm not going to go camping with those people. We all navigate the world through humor, everybody does. And yet most of that vanishes, it disappears. How many times in every person's life have they saved a terrible situation with humor? Like making a child laugh who's crying over something. So much of that stuff disappears.

My first big cultural heroes were comedians: Steve Martin, George Carlin, and Richard Pryor. I had their records, I memorized them. I knew

Monty Python and Firesign Theater by heart. I think in my own life, it was a way of handling pain. I like art where I can feel the artist trying to reach me. Humor is one of the ways that you can sense the artist saying, "I got something for you." And there's a lot of art that isn't like that.

RS I'm interested in humor in art not being taken seriously. You said humor is this thing that has saved so many of us, and it brings us pleasure. Why then is it off limits, as the subject of a work of art?

TD Maybe for photography it's all a vestige of some kind of older thing about the medium. I wrote this essay about photography and humor in particular, about how photographers have always felt second-rate. They need their own special galleries sometimes. Or like in the slide library at the Yale Art Gallery, there were categories like "Sculpture" and "Painting," and then there were "Minor Arts," which included photography.

RS A little inferiority complex?

TD Yeah. I think with photographers, you have to measure up. I think there's also a whole other thing, editorial photography, and the idea of a sense of purpose. And it has to be this self-righteous, concerned photography.

I think that the comedians of the times are the philosophers of the times. Somebody like George Carlin, who is basically reckoning with the meaning of language. He's somebody that if you really wanted to take a measure of what his cultural time was, you just listen to him. And it would tell you more than lots of essayists. And today, it's people like Dave Chappelle—he had these two comedy specials last year that were just deeply profound. And delivered in a way that's consumable. That's another complicated thing. Humor and music are ways in which the delivery system of the work is a little bit more palatable.

RS Why do you think narrative is important for us as humans and how is it also maybe our downfall?

TD I don't believe that it's possible to experience the world in a non-narrative way. There is no way to experience language without narrative.

Light Comedy Grave Rubbings, 2018
17 works, crayon on paper
Installation dimensions variable
Installation view, Tang Museum, Saratoga Springs, New York, 2018

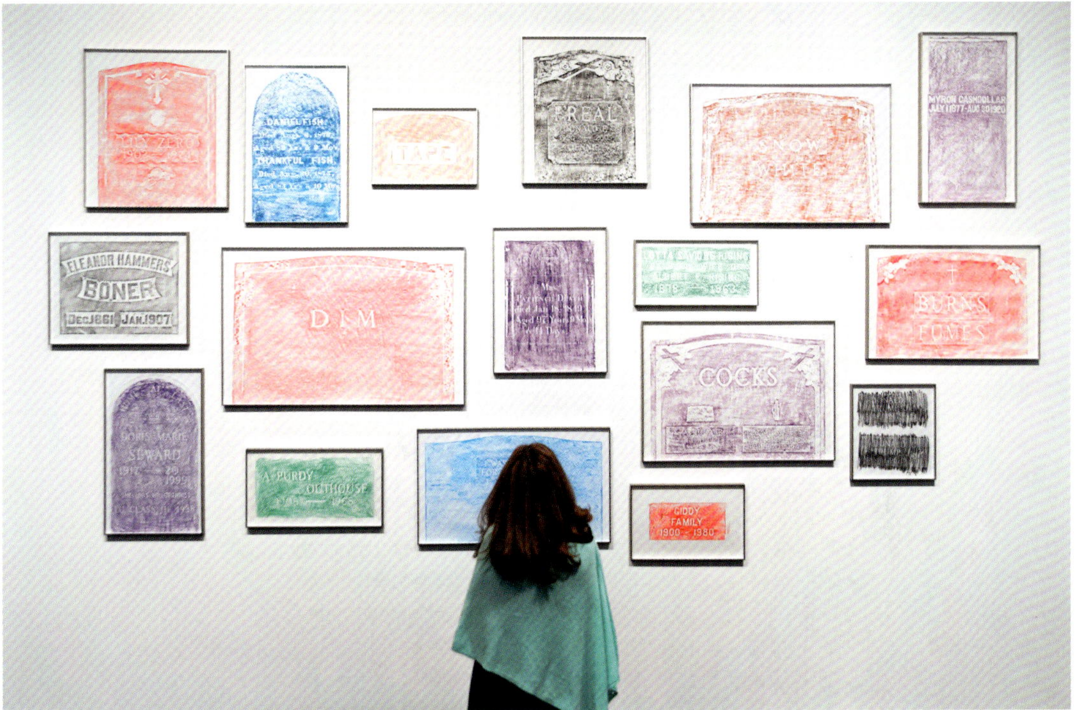

If you randomly pick up any two words and you put them together, no matter how disjunctive they are, you create a little narrative. They bounce off of each other and they create friction and bonds start to form between them. I also believe very strongly that narrative is the thing that makes us human as opposed to animals. I really believe that storytelling is what makes us who we are. And art comes from that.

RS What are your thoughts on the American dream?

TD It's alive and well! I feel super patriotic about America. Part of it is that everything I do is a little bit contingent on the fact that nobody is paying much attention to much of what's going on, in that we don't live in a codified culture where you know what your place is. I feel privileged and special to be able to pay attention to the things I pay attention to. The American dream is a little bit dependent on a kind of alienation where you don't know your place. I have never felt like I really had a home. I never felt that I necessarily had a people. I've never had any money and I've never had too many connections. But I've always felt like I can make whatever I want to make out of whatever I can get a hold of. And that feels really thrilling.

RS I consider the subject matter of much of your work to be the American dream. Do you see it that way?

TD Yeah. I mean, I've always been really surprised at all the discussion about religion in this country and yet I don't think this is a profoundly religious place compared to other places. And I don't think that even the people who are claiming to be religious really are. But I think it's obvious that the most powerful religion is daily life; the pleasures of daily life and that people know how to enjoy themselves and take comfort in small acts of daily existence. I am drawn to places that are not succeeding by traditional measures of the American dream necessarily.

In a way, despite everything that's said about Americans being close-minded and self-interested, the reality is that we live in this open way where we're available and can be seen by lots of people—on our front porches and in our suburban back yards and most people don't have a fence. That's my American dream.

RS How would you characterize this exhibition?

TD It's a kind of fun house with lots of sensory information—maybe a little overstuffed. There's an aspect of the humor in it which is a little unsettling. I don't mind making somebody feel a little bit uncomfortable. For example, *Uneasy Listening* is both funny and a bit difficult to listen to. These things might not all be the most profound things in the world, but they feel really important somehow.

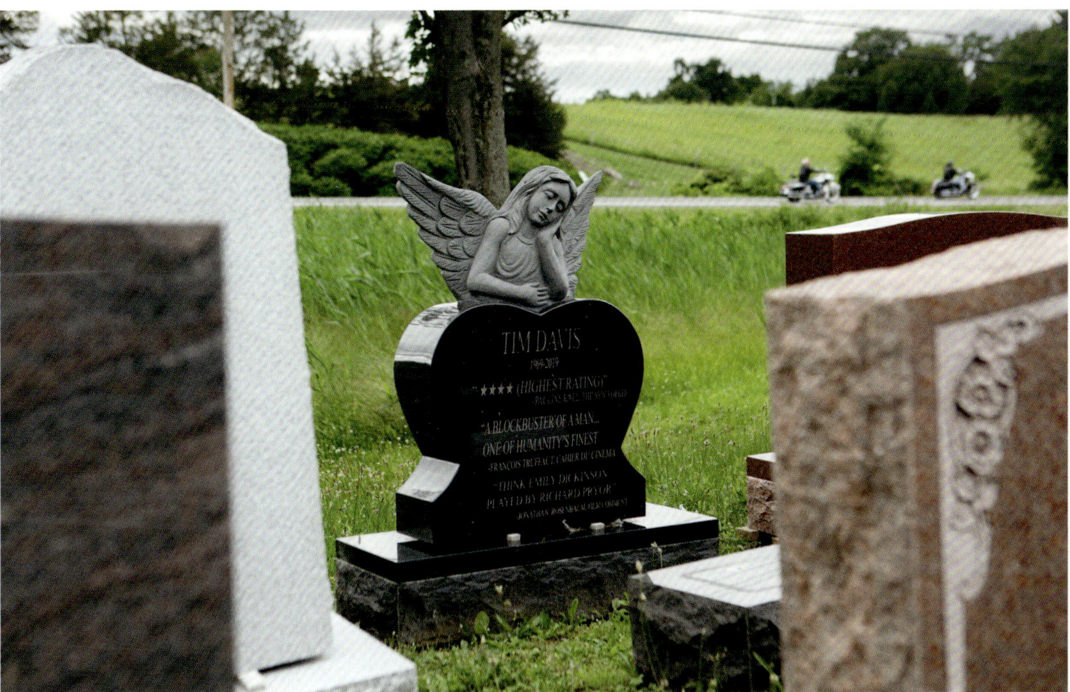

My Gravestone
from *Cartoons*, 2018
Archival inkjet print
24 x 30 inches

RS Sometimes you are showing us things that might not be the most important things in the world but they are really important for us to see.

TD Cleverness is something I value. And it's another thing that's marginalized and considered kind of louche. But it's really important. The grave rubbings, for example. If you're walking through a graveyard and some of the names are funny, you should do something with that. If you really want to explain who I am as an artist, here it is: He's in a graveyard, he sees a funny name and thinks, "I want to make a grave rubbing of this." I'm a photographer, so my initial instinct would be to take a picture of it but then I thought, "you know, I can use a cultural form that already exists to make something that will totally upset our expectations." It's definitely not being proper, right? It's not the reverent thing to do to laugh at somebody's name.

And yet, in the show, there's also my own gravestone. My own funny gravestone, that I made because I wouldn't want it any other way. Do you want people to cry for the rest of their lives that you're gone? No, you don't. You want them to remember you with the joyous things and the things that make you laugh.

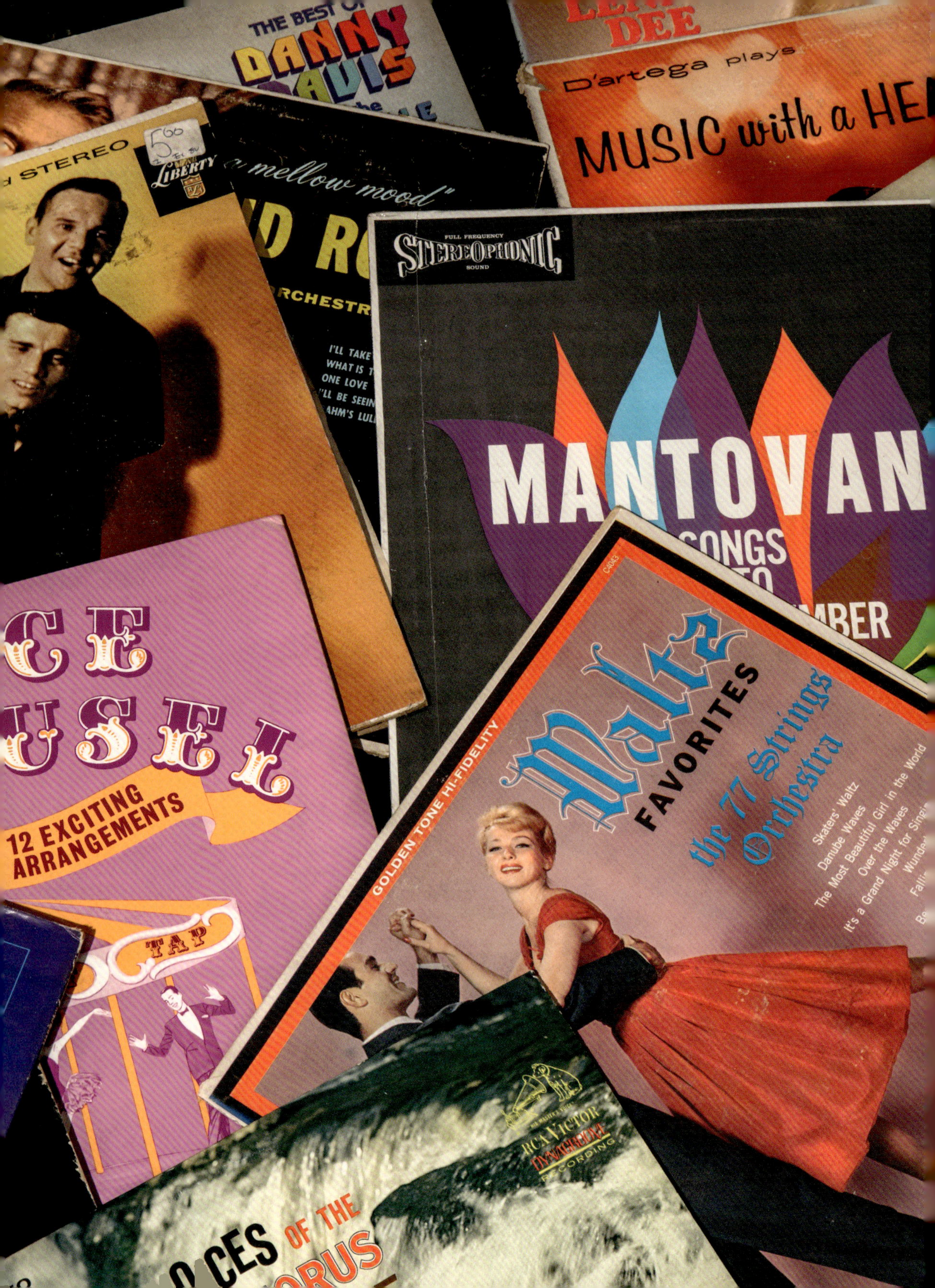

DANNY
DAVIS
DEE
D'artega plays
STEREO
LIBERTY
"a mellow mood"
FULL FREQUENCY
STEREOPHONIC
SOUND
12 EXCITING ARRANGEMENTS
TAP
GOLDEN TONE HI-FIDELITY
Waltz
FAVORITES
the 77 Strings Orchestra
Skaters' Waltz
Danube Waves
The Most Beautiful Girl in the World
Over the Waves
RCA Victor
OF THE

A HUNTER AND A GATHERER

LUC SANTE

TIM DAVIS IS NOT SO MUCH A STREET PHOTOGRAPHER as a road photographer. He goes about his work the old-fashioned way, by hunting and gathering, and he finds wild and unexpected combinations of color, form, and meaning just sitting there on the roadside where anyone could have seen them, but nobody else did. He is an aesthete, an exacting technician, a connoisseur of all the incongruities in the semi-domesticated American landscape—and of course he is a collector. Every photographer is some kind of collector, but Tim doesn't just collect with his camera. He collects images however he can get them, also sounds, jokes, performances, artifacts of every sort. And he is a very particular sort of collector: Like Aby Warburg or Otto Bettman, he is a typologist. He thinks in series, and he thinks big.

He enjoys the feeling of sheer physical accumulation. The first project-related request I can recall getting from him was for vinyl copies—condition unimportant—of Bob Dylan's *Self Portrait*. I didn't have any, but I was interested: How in fact was he going to make a self-portrait, as he promised, from those *Self Portraits*? The answer: a stack as high as the top of his head. That is a goal he may or may not have achieved, but it's the mass of the thing that counts. It would hurt if it fell on you. He has also collected the single deadest genre of twentieth-century American music: the programmatic glop—vocal, orchestral, quasi-jazz, pseudo-Latin—that was the musical equivalent of couch art, the stuff people bought in the 50s and early 60s when they had a fancy new record player but not a clue as to what kind of music to play on it. It was a segment of American cultural production that died unmourned

Uneasy Listening (detail), 2018
Mixed media
Dimensions variable

long ago but remains ubiquitous in the secondary markets, precisely because no one has any use for it. Anybody who goes out looking for old records will be confronted by massive accretions of the stuff, some of it continuously on display for over half a century. You can imagine Davis's glee at having an excuse to adopt those long-term orphans and then redistribute them, foisting them on museum visitors—who will, at length, feed them right back into the Goodwill supply chain.

Davis is a joker and an anthropologist. The comedy of the *Library of Ideas* rests on accumulation, but it also represents a philosophical inquiry pursued through hundreds of hours of field work—yet again in the garage sales and thrift shops of the nation, those places where onetime personal attempts at innovation or enlightenment go to die or await reincarnation. *Light Comedy Grave Rubbings* presumably cost the artist hundreds of hours on findagrave.com in addition to the travel time and rubbing labor. Graveyards are the junk shop of lineage, the repository of family names that have died out or been changed due to embarrassment. The collecting ventures resulting in the library and the grave rubbings both involved surveying a territory as vast as the country but nevertheless limited by actuality. Davis clearly welcomes the constraint, but as the *Cartoons* show, he can be impatient with the demands of mere facts. Being an artist, of course, he can simply supply his own. If it seems surprising that nowhere in the vastness of the nation does there appear to be a chair store called *Shack of Sit*, he will create it himself.

The most anthropologically rigorous works in the show are *Curtain Calls* and *Counting In*, which document ancient rituals that may never have been observed quite that way before. Each ritual has its ostensible purpose: the theater troupe assembles in full to solicit applause; the leader of the musical combo establishes the time signature while also calling the band members to attention. Viewed as a chain of brief performances by a variety of outfits, dissociated from context, they reveal their singular dramatic qualities. The curtain call becomes a line dance, the count-in a tense, minimalist existential play employing only four words of text. The curtain call rejoices in extravagant costuming;

the count-in pretends its actors aren't wearing costumes at all. The curtain callers are middle-aged and beaming; the counters-in are young and miserable.

It's Okay to Hate Yourself, which runs on a medium-sized monitor, shows brilliantly destabilizing images, apparently sequenced to keep viewers on their toes as they flit from indoor to outdoor, day to night, long shot to close-up, humor to sadness to bewilderment. *South Sea Selfies* are presented true to their nature—on a smartphone at the end of a selfie stick—which makes them easy to overlook and mildly irritating to view, especially since their gloriously sensuous expansiveness must be conjured via a screen the size of a bar of hotel soap. They are expert parodies of the selfie, showing Davis inserting himself, often ridiculously, into the daily activities and incomparable vistas of Bali. Every one of them is nevertheless a small miracle of lighting, composition, physical ingenuity—it's hard to account for how some of them might have been shot, and were they even taken on a smart phone?—and comedic performance. Davis has constructed a persona as an oblivious tourist, somewhere between Jacques Tati and Harold Lloyd, who strikes incongruous poses in the foregrounds of scenes that magnificently refuse to absorb him. It's a *tour de force*, presenting a foreign culture by highlighting the outsider's awkwardness, making the observer's paradox the framing device. It may be the heart of the show, and yet Davis has purposefully made it easy to overlook. Davis is a collector and an artist and a joker and a trickster, and his show is a Wunderkabinett.

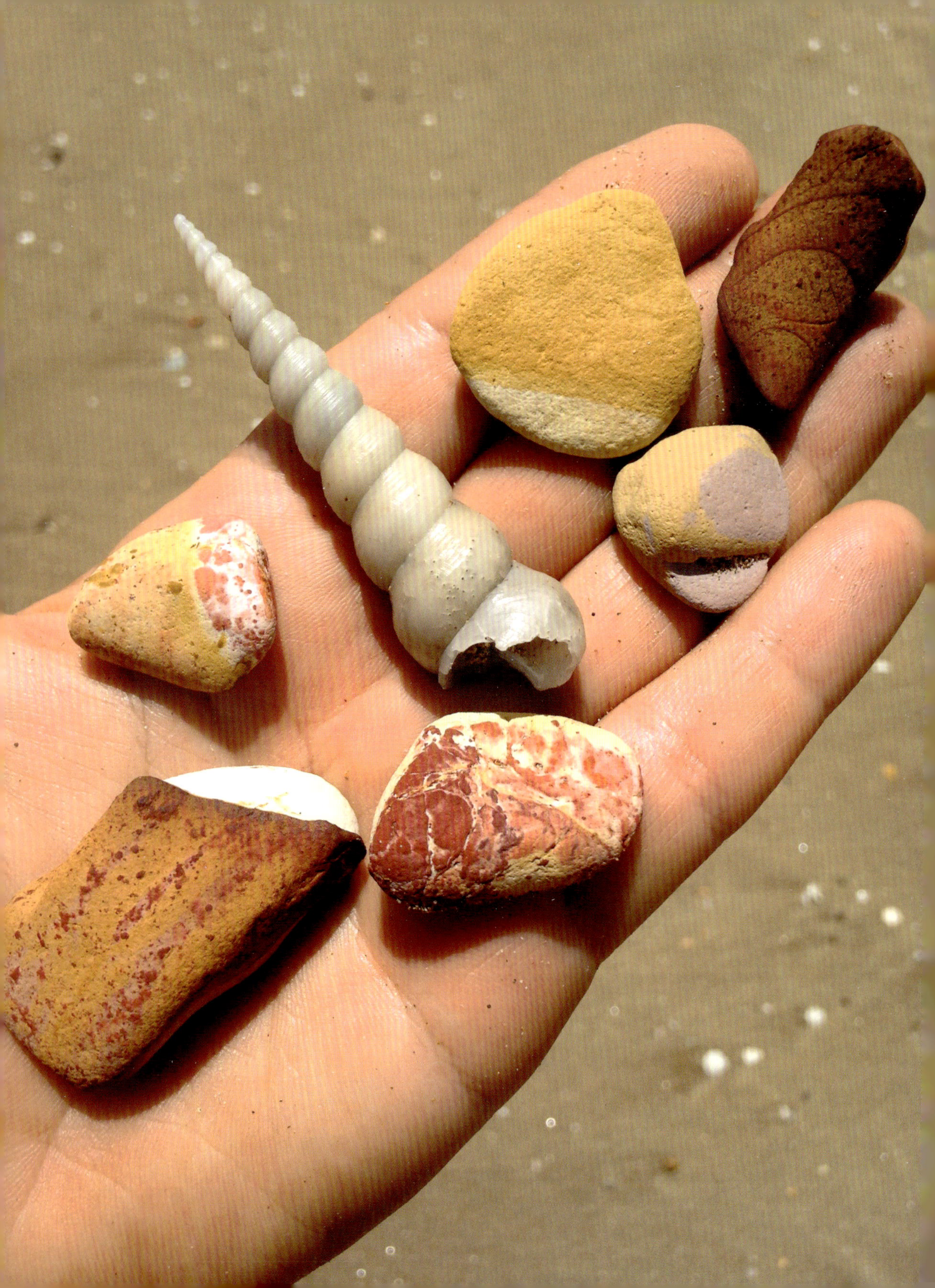

PORTABLE HOLE

TIM DAVIS

THESIS

I KNOW WHERE I BECAME A COLLECTOR. I could pretend I know when, but I'd be guessing, and looking very deep within, at a little boy in love with dinosaurs, in love with knowing about dinosaurs, in love with knowing. Knowing that there were gingko trees in dinosaur times, and that the tree down at the end of the block, in the strange side yard of a once-elegant rooming house, is a gingko tree. It was there I became a collector. The same splendid green fans scattered on the grass that were flattened under the Allosauruses as they reared up menacingly. We now think the T. Rex and his three-fingered cousin, the Allosaurus, were likely scavengers, who fell forward low to the ground instead of rearing up. Growing up means watching your myths get unlivable. But the little collector still lives in his myth. He's maybe three, under the great corner gingko, reaching out for a Luna moth-shaped (and colored!) leaf and knowing, "I know about this." I'd learned to read at two. I must've been cascaded with smiles and displayed to neighbors. Adored. The ginkgo leaf is the bottled feeling of still being in the myth; the myth of Mommy and Daddy and me, and of endless possibility. We live on this block and this block is my range, my world to explore. Memorizing every sidewalk square, the slate ones (smooth, multicolored, irregular, interesting) and the poured concrete (embossed with very recent fossils—a footprint, sometimes even a gingko leaf). There's a kind of halfway house halfway down the block producing some Appalachian dissonance. And anyway, the whole town is a creepy Victorian spookhouse where our friends live in raccoon-filled gothic cottages with no running water. And I'm not scared

South Sea Selfies (detail), 2017
Digital photographs, iPod, selfie stick
Dimensions variable

to walk all the way to the gingko tree. Even though I'm only three. And I am brave enough to turn into the strange yard and pick up a gingko leaf and put it in my pocket. I'm not scared of dinosaurs. I know about them.

ANTITHESIS

The Funsters are playing Dungeons & Dragons in the basement of a raised ranch down a divorce-scented cul-de-sac. The Funsters are home alone after school. We've just finished making a comedy sketch tape. I have invented a character named John Zimbabwe Ahhhhhh who is some sort of detective, but I can't stop cracking up whenever I say, "John Zimbabwe Ahhhhhh," and I'm ruining the tape but it's so funny that the whole sketch is just preteen boys laughing till they can't breathe and still trying to say their lines, and you'll never hear anything funnier. I'd never be able to say it but I knew even then that true friends are the most important collection you make. The ones you admire enough to copy their affect, read their books, listen to their records. The Funsters were theatrical and clever. They were Anglophiles: Monty Python, Brian Eno. They built their own myth, and it was resonant to hide inside theirs, mine having been long shattered.

I ruined the D&D, too: too much protocol. Whatever the opposite of protocol is, it governs me. You have to roll a nineteen or above to use the potion. You can't access the portal without finding the key. I couldn't take it. Fun game—got dragons in it—but all these rules, and all you're really doing is math. The game should be called "Math in a Dungeon." I knew it wasn't for me. My people are impulsive, vivid, off-kilter, desperate for attention, utterly out of step with everyone around them. My grandfather would ask any maître d' or stranger, "Where's the ladies' room?" It was a running joke that set so much protocol afire. It was flirty: "I'm not like the others, are you with me?" But it was dirty: "Now, mentally reconsider my gender." Where is the bathroom? is the second question you learn in any foreign language and my grandfather wielded

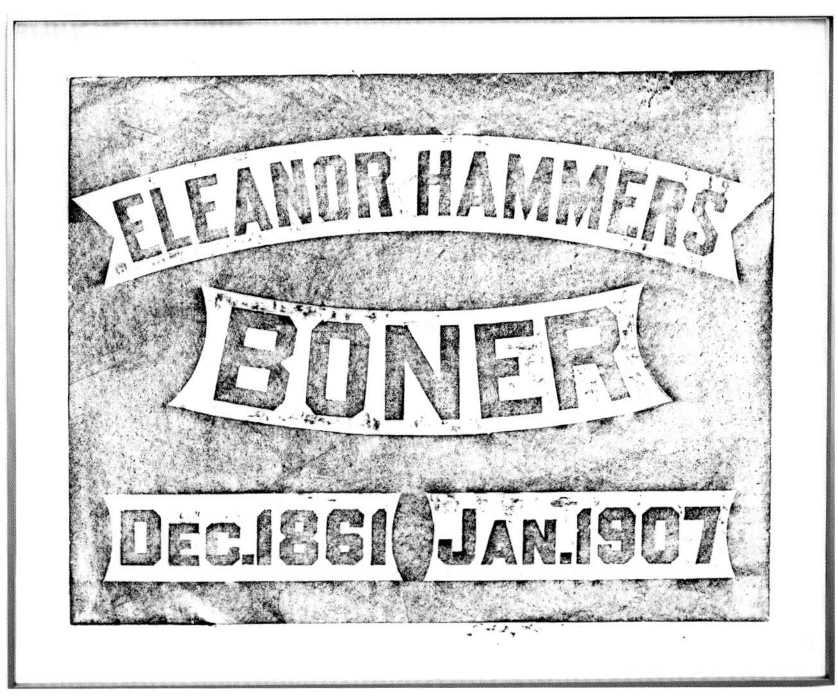

Boner from *Light Comedy Grave Rubbings*, 2017
Crayon on paper
28 x 23 inches

it like a stiletto, slicing and dicing the sails of protocol. Language is protocol. It's how we all agree to speak. Watch my people misguide and undermine. Listen as they tip the canoe of agreement over. Listen.

> *Pizzeria worker: Here you go, sir. One large and one small cheese.*
> *My father: Thank you, severely.*

The Funsters are playing Dungeons & Dragons and the one thing I collect from the game are the clever ways its makers repaired rips in the sail of protocol. Take, for example, the portable hole. You spend the first part of this grand adventure shopping. Shopping is not exciting. I prefer toilet cleaning to shopping. The founders of this game thought, "Fighting! But first, Shopping!!!" You're a knight on a long quest. You need armor and weapons and stuff; too much stuff to carry. So, you can buy a "portable hole," a bottomless pit that fits in your pocket, holding all your plundered booty. Someday we'll all have portable holes in our pockets that will pillage our time and attention. But for now, I fill my portable hole with failures of protocol. Real giddy glee rises up in things that don't fit, in seeing things the wrong way 'round. I know I don't fit. I know cleverness and unswallowable laughter can save the Funsters from worrying over their single mothers and near poverty. Collecting is the opposite of playing a game. You make your own rules. Poverty is impossible. The world is littered with value.

PARENTHESIS

I'm writing this in the Asbury Park Public Library. It's a magnificent building, built for a private literary club. There's an enormous stained-glass window of Ulysses S. Grant, who died during its construction. "He lived to see peace and harmony restored in his country," is how it is inscribed, on a long, folded ruby glass ribbon. I hope my stained-glass window says the same. Facing west is another window, this one by Tiffany. As the sun sets, the flames on a burning Viking ship come alive. There's a Longfellow poem rolling like credits below:

> *They launched the burning ship!*
> *It floated far away*
> *Over the misty sea,*
> *Till like the sun it seemed,*
> *Sinking beneath the waves.*[1]

A burning ship sinking beneath the waves? Remind you of anything?

---

1 Henry Wadsworth Longfellow, "Tegnér's Drapa," 1847.

There are still books on shelves here (and a physical card catalog!) but the most vivid function of the public library today is as a soup kitchen for the Internet. An elderly queen is having problems logging into his Yahoo. He speaks prep-school Spanish to the librarian, who is trying to retrieve his password. I hear him guess, "Cherubim1234?" A woman with a Liberian accent needs help with her CV. A middle-aged man is watching Bruce Springsteen videos on YouTube. He's on his thirteenth or fourteenth in a row. I collect this man. He's everything to me, everything funny and tragic and literary and off color and particular. What is he doing here? If this is not a question you ask every second you move through the world, you're either enlightened or incurious. I smile. Maybe the New Jersey statehouse has passed a program to hire suffering people to increase Springsteen's Internet profile. They are sent out to public libraries to increase the number of his streams. It's good business for the state, protecting a valuable resource and helping the needy, an Intellectual Property Peace Corps. Big smiles. I should be writing this essay about collecting, and what collecting means to my artistic practice. Instead, I write the theme song of the New Jersey Springsteen Corps.

Baby Bruce, you was the golden goose who satisfied our dreams
Born to Run went to Number One in the nineteen seventies
Synthesizers colonized ya, sounding like a-doodle-a-day
That didn't stop ya selling papa Born in the USA

And now I'm JACKING UP YOUR STREAMS, JACKING UP YOUR STREAMS
I work for the government, JACKING UP YOUR STREAMS

In my head, the song sounds like "Walk This Way" if played by The Kinks. It shakes your booty and makes you smile. I rush into the stacks snorting with laughter. I'm in a public library, laughing uncontrollably while the burning ship sinks beneath the waves.

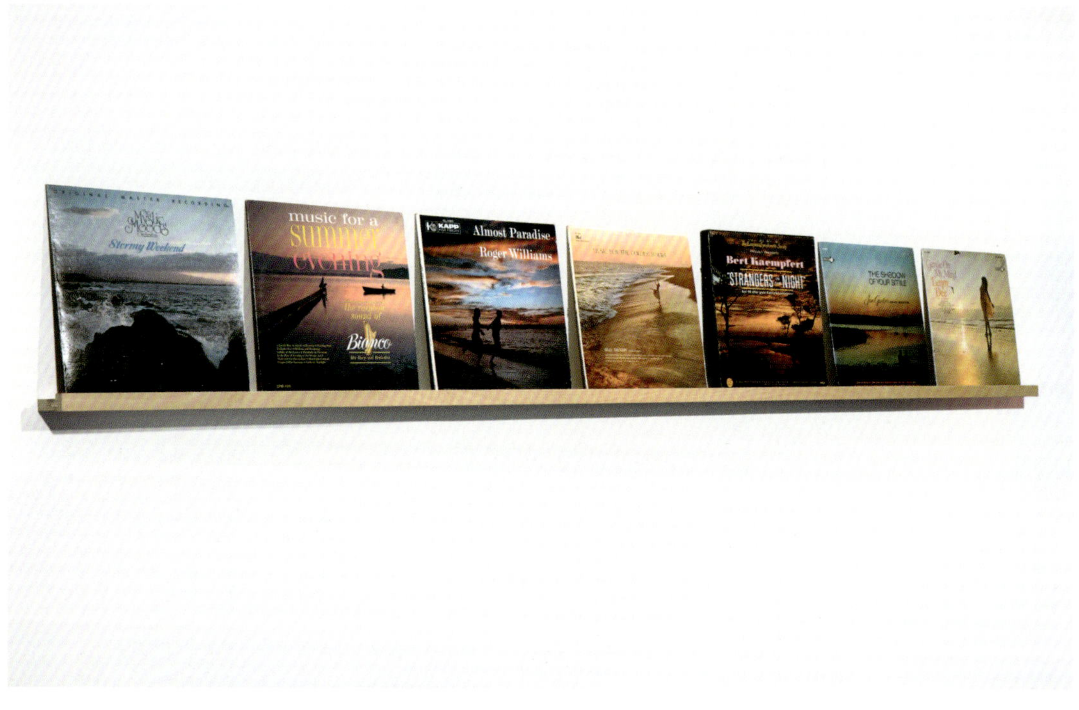

Uneasy Listening
(detail), 2018
Mixed media
Dimensions variable
Installation view,
Tang Museum,
Saratoga Springs,
New York, 2018

PROSTHESIS

My father has a darkroom off the kitchen (to this day I get instantly famished when I smell fixer) and I'm curious. He loads me up his Olympus OM-1 and I walk toward the corner gingko. The camera is a portable hole, gathering dozens of dioramas, landscapes, patches of light, people you can't take your eyes off of. Every picture you take is an assertion of your certainty, a display of your knowledge and awareness, a rung you've clung to on the ladder out of ambivalence and doubt. Every picture you take is a stone in your own foundation, and yet it occupies almost no space. It weighs less than a gingko leaf.

I float through the neighborhood, instinctively drawn to ways the late day summer sun thickens the details of the strange old houses. Being *drawn to* is the essence of being a collector, feeling the gravity of the outer world, and letting it pull you in. But a picture isn't a burden, so gravity releases you as soon as you've clicked the shutter, reborn. I feel *drawn to*, and drawn *forth*. The collector loves to move, to sift through stuff in search of. I cross the street, beyond what had been the limit of my reach, and down the next block. I'm older now—nine or ten—back here in this town, visiting my father for the summer, partial custody in the myth. This venerable resort destination has as many alleys as streets. Alleys, built for grooms and servants, leave backyards naked and exposed, feinting past the carnival show of a house's façade. There's a thrill in it, swimming through the membrane of public and private and seeing what you're not supposed to, and an incredulity that others don't see. Three yards down the first one I stop in my tracks. A man is on his back porch, in a samurai sword slice of light, feeding a big white dog from a bottle. A bicentennial American flag, with the cute curly 76, hangs from an enormous copper beech. I see the scene. I recognize its obvious limits and know that what I see is a picture. I slip it in my portable hole. Now I walk down every alley I come to, feeling like I'm in a hidden world, a Narnia or Secret Garden, or that dream where there are uncharted rooms in your apartment. I've started a new collection and it's somehow steadying and unsettling, like building your own myth.

SYNAESTHESIS

In the recurring dream I wake up from a dream. I'm staring at the white ceiling of a white room, vaguely longer than square. There are white curtains hanging at the edges of vision but I can't follow them down to see what's out the windows. I now realize that I am paralyzed, and that all I'll ever see is this parallelogram of white. I am destroyed with despair. I've woken up in a ruined world. No accident or meningitis comes to mind. All that comes is the certainty that everything that's made me *me* is gone forever. Me is over. I can't cry but I am dipped in bitterness. All I can do is go back to sleep.

I wake up again, this time at night, to the same hideous persistence of vision. I try holding my breath to see if you can suicide that way. You can't. I didn't imagine this could get worse, but night makes everything worse. Then a car passes by outside, and its headlights make a beam pass across the ceiling in a delirious elliptical sweep. Soon another passes, and another. The lights play over my field of vision, as rare and tempting as the aurora, as comforting as a lighthouse to a listing ship. I am charged awake, filled with gratefulness and grace, knowing there will always be enough to see.

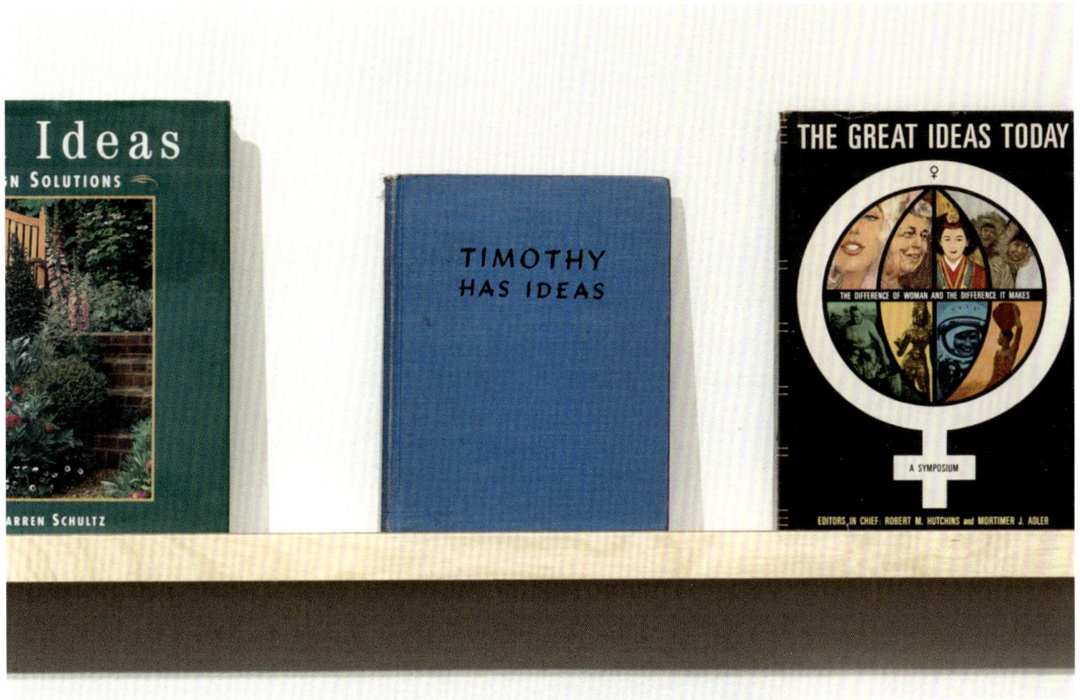

Library of Ideas
(detail), 2018
Mixed media
Dimensions variable
Installation view,
Tang Museum, Saratoga
Springs, New York, 2018

(following spread)

It's OK to Hate
Yourself, 2015
Video
43 minutes
Installation view, Tang
Museum, Saratoga
Springs, New York, 2018

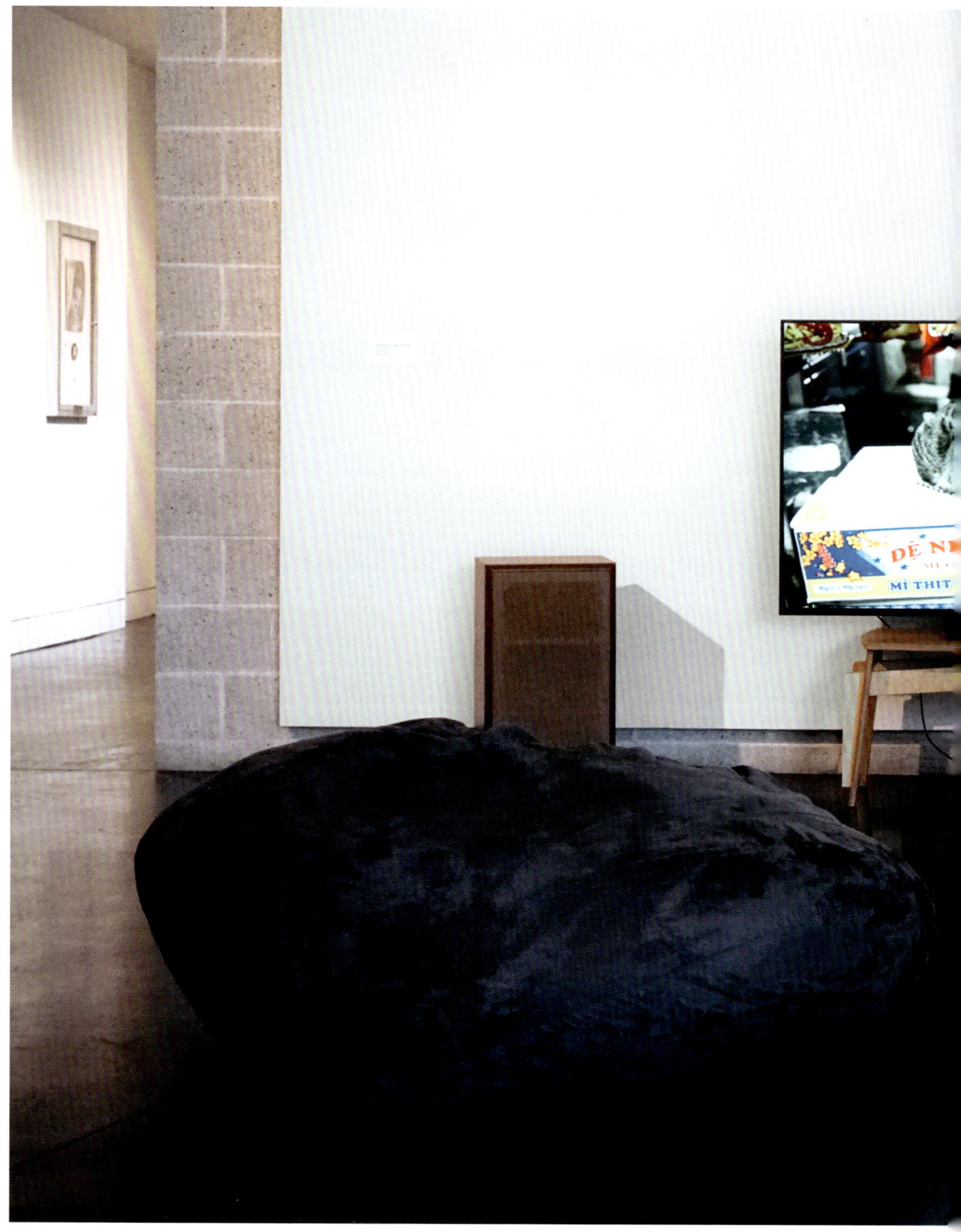

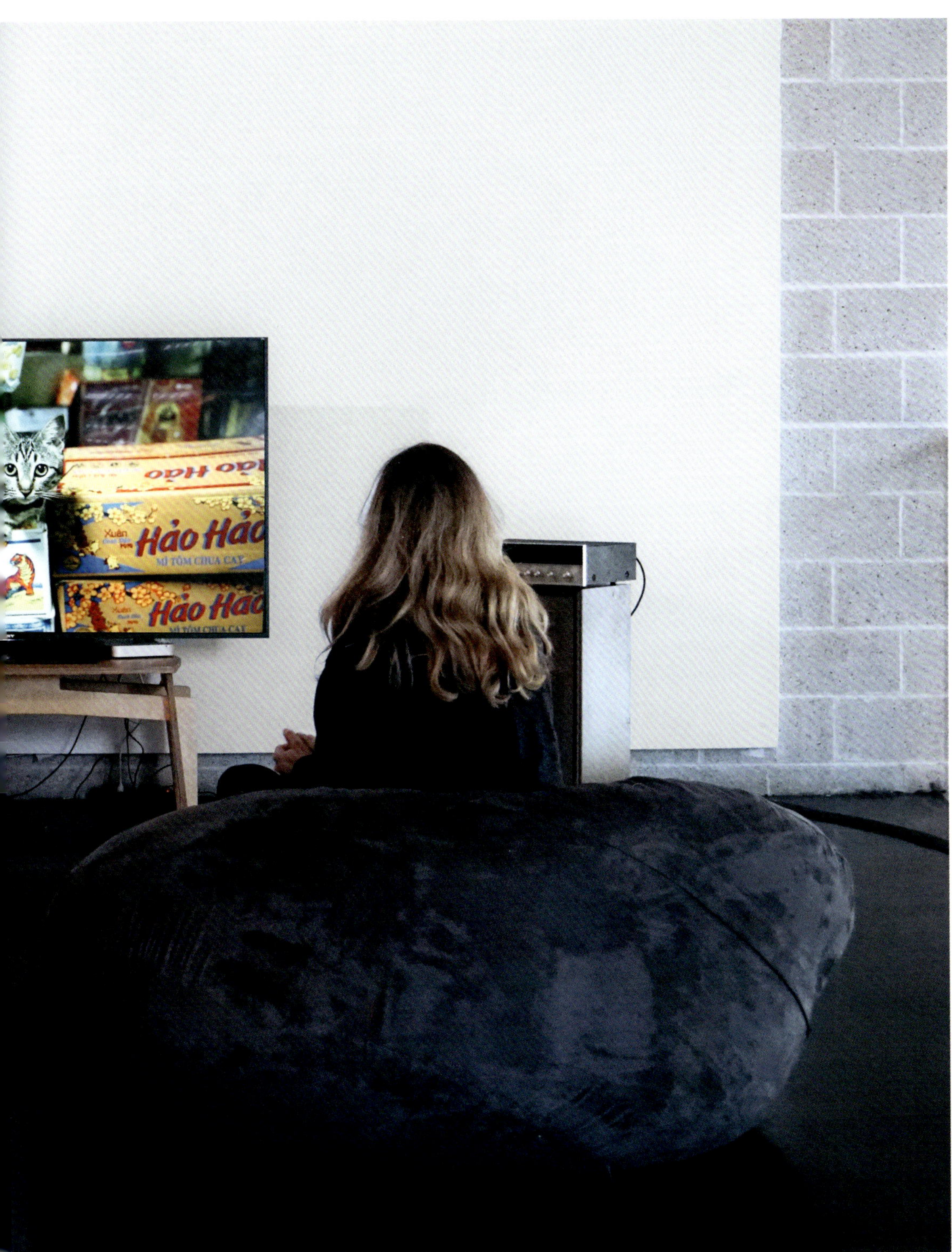
Xuân
MÌ TÔM CHUA CAY

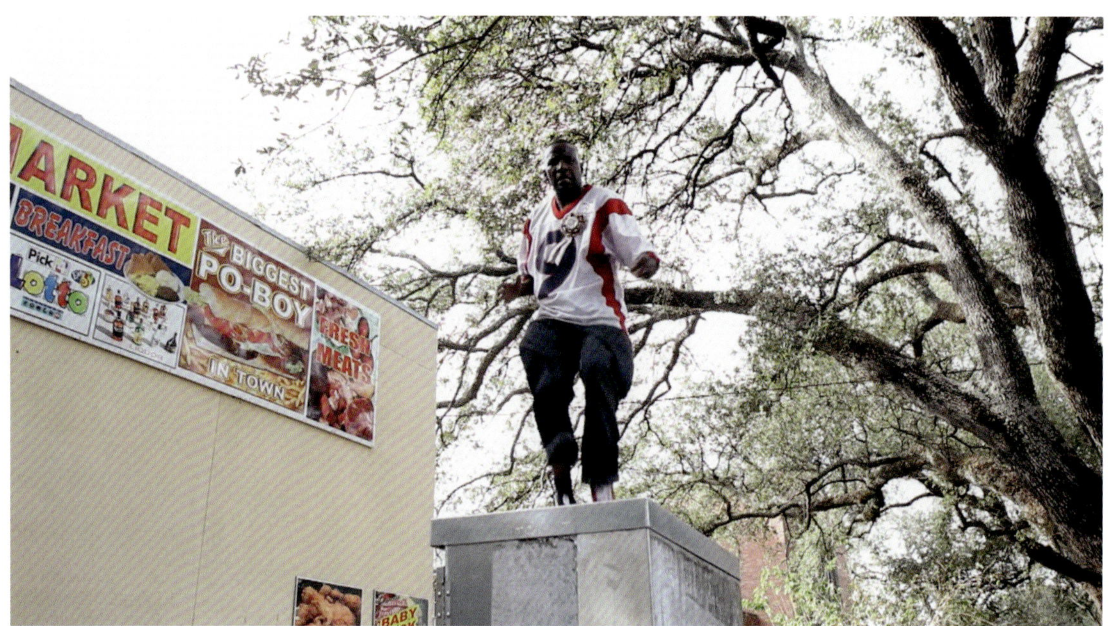
MARKET
BREAKFAST
Pick
Lotto
THE BIGGEST
PO-BOY
IN TOWN
FRESH
MEATS
BABY

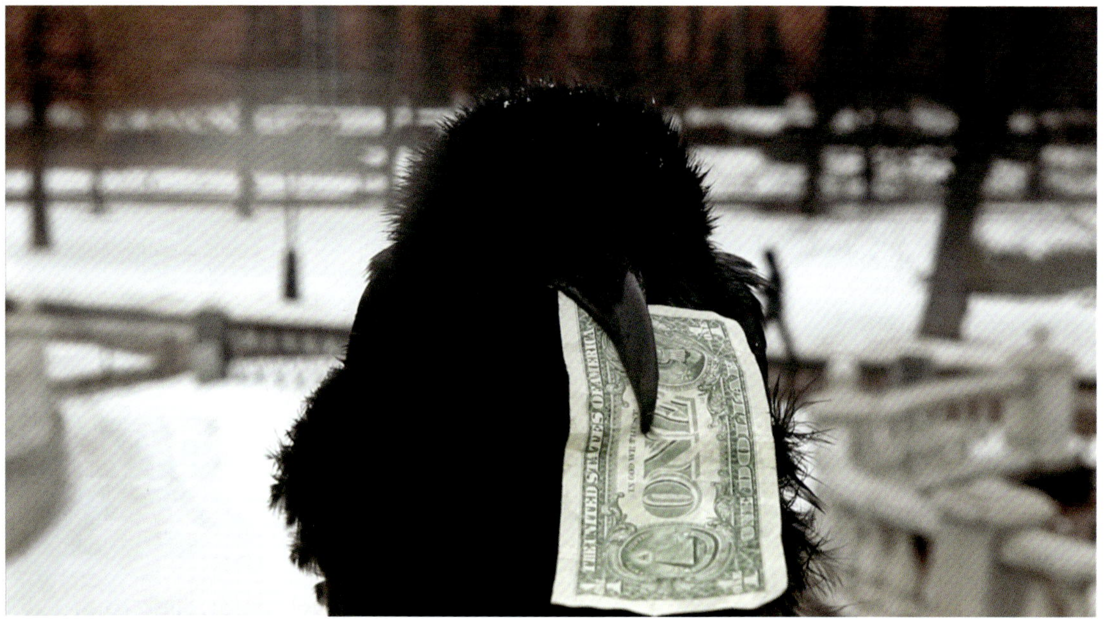

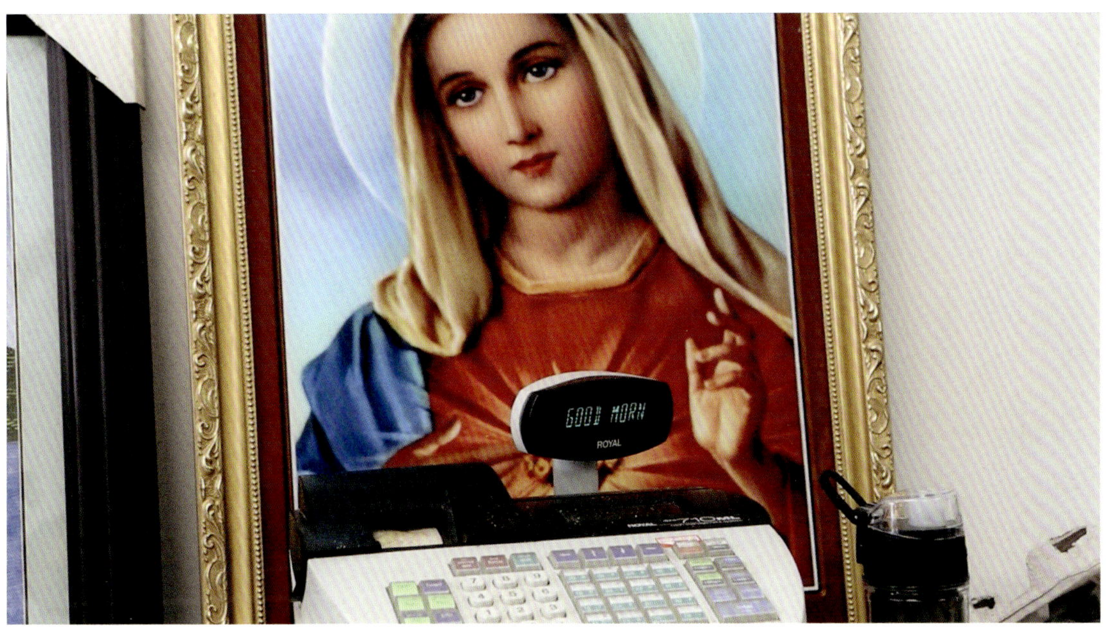

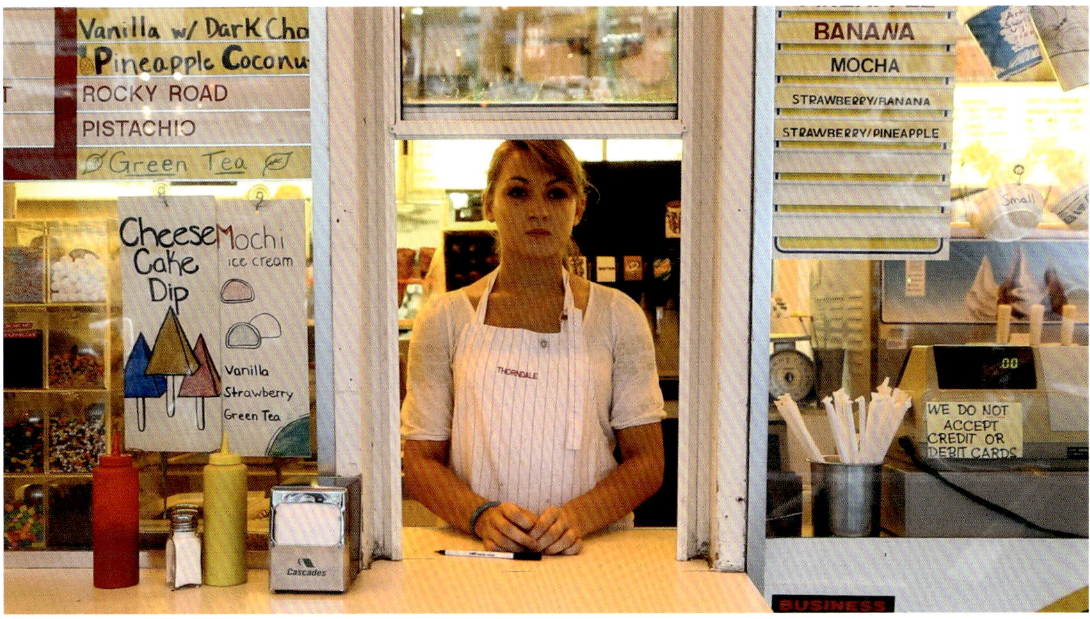

It's OK to Hate Yourself, 2015
(video stills)
Video
43 minutes

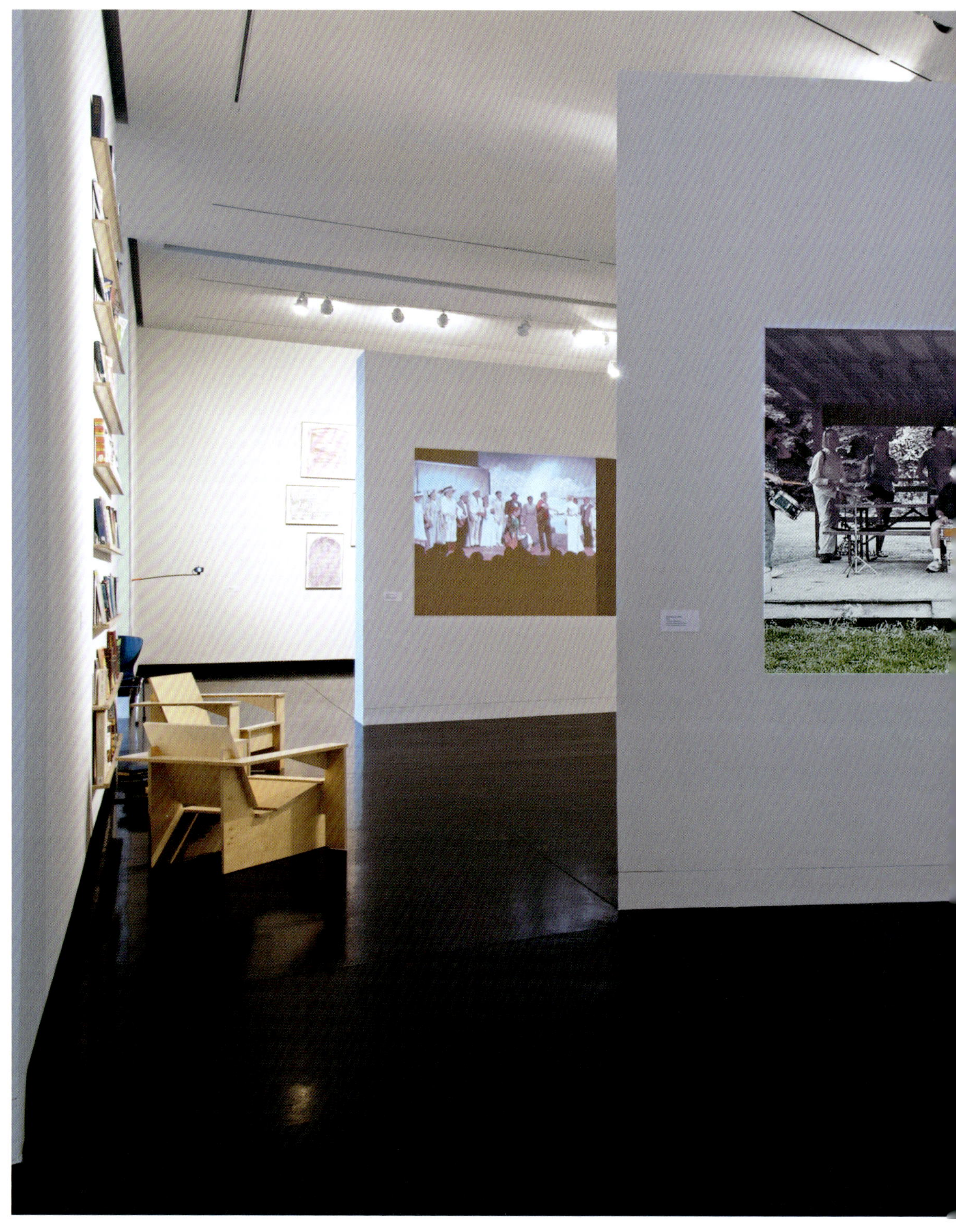

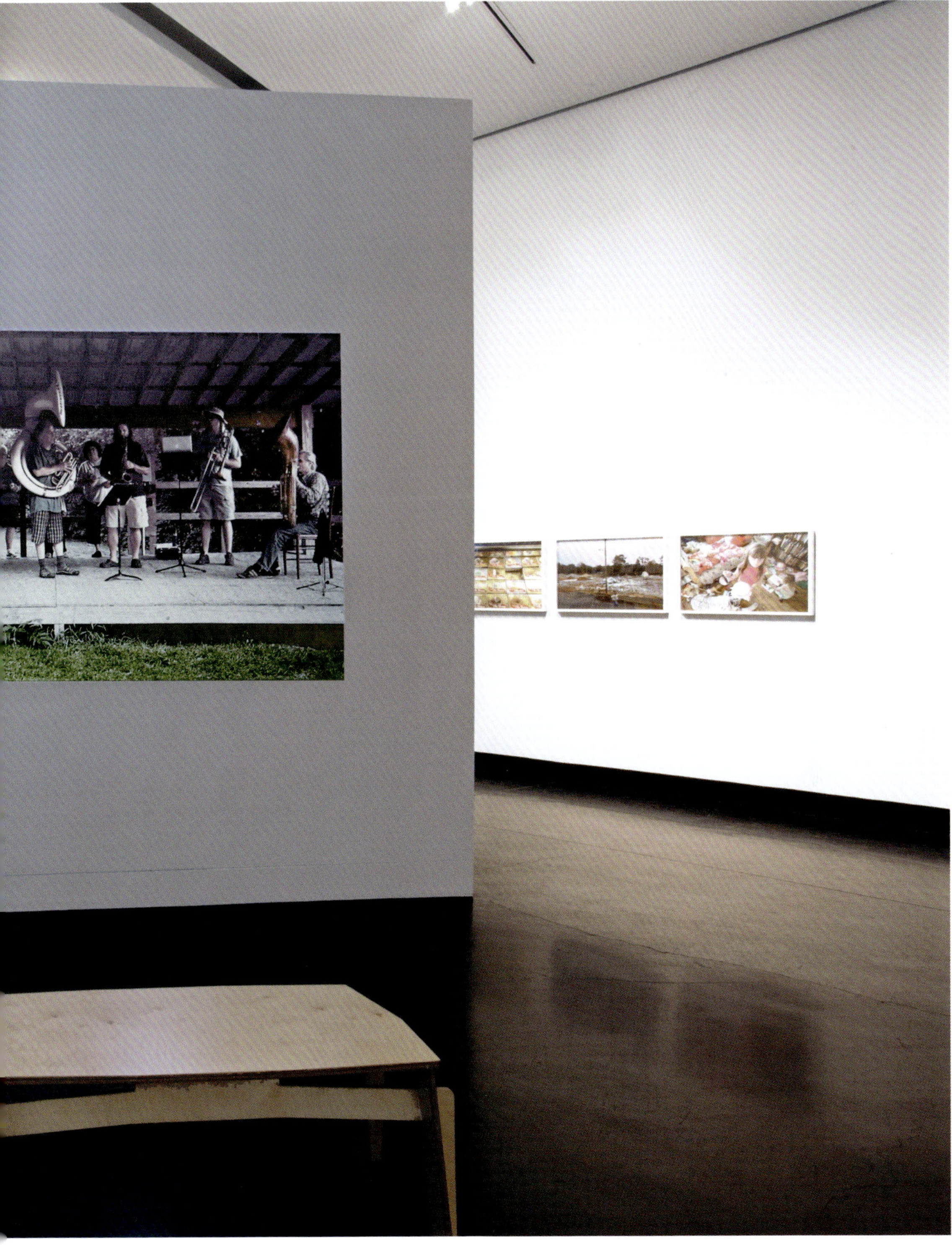

(previous spread)

Installation view with *Counting In*, 2015, video, 3 minutes, 30 seconds
Tang Museum, Saratoga Springs, New York, 2018

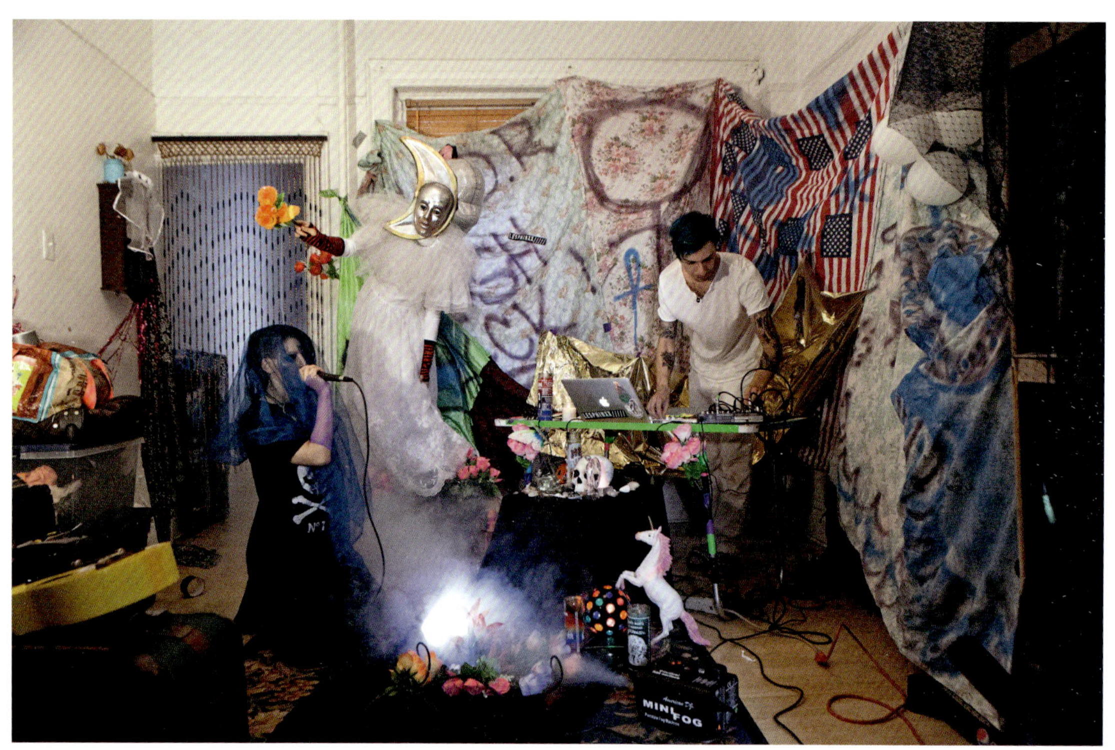

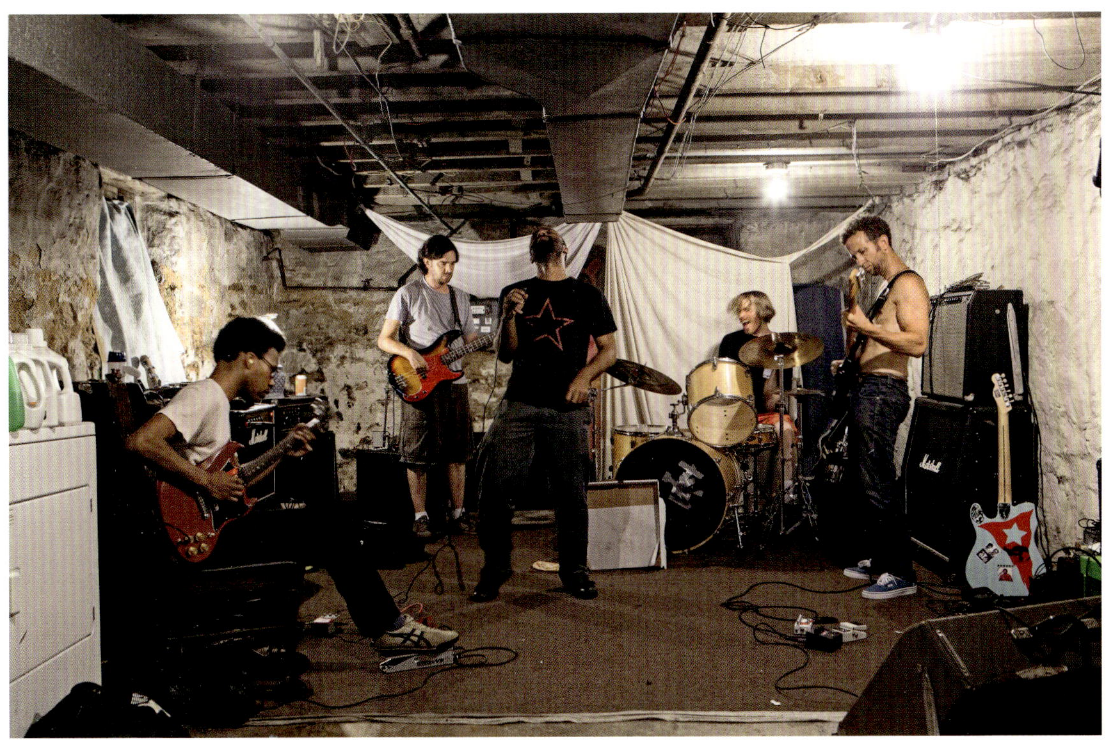

(above and facing)

Counting In, 2015
(video stills)
Video
3 minutes, 30 seconds

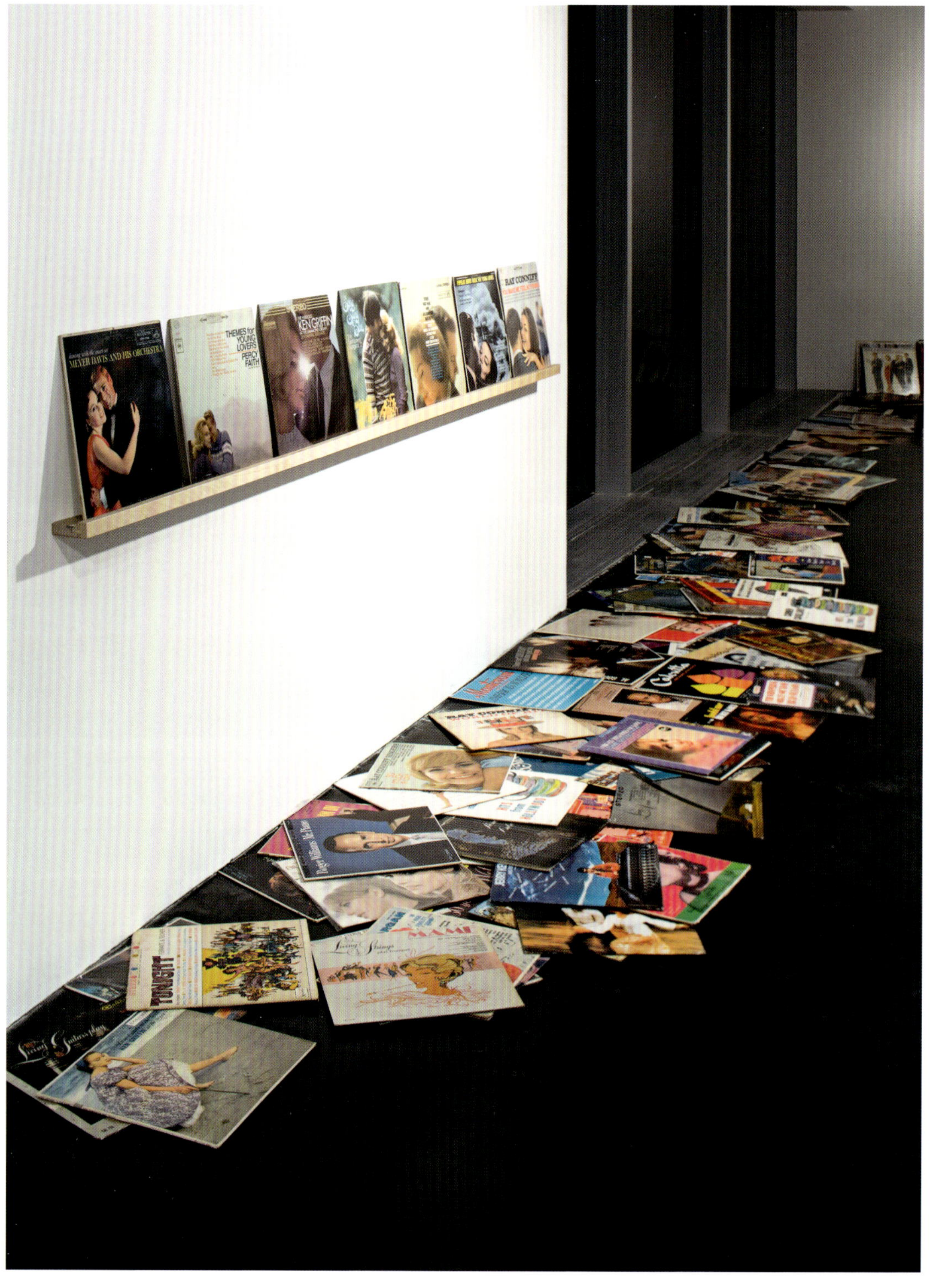
MEYER DAVIS AND HIS ORCHESTRA
THEMES for YOUNG LOVERS
PERCY FAITH
KEN GRIFFIN
RAY CONNIFF
TONIGHT
Roger Williams Mr. Piano

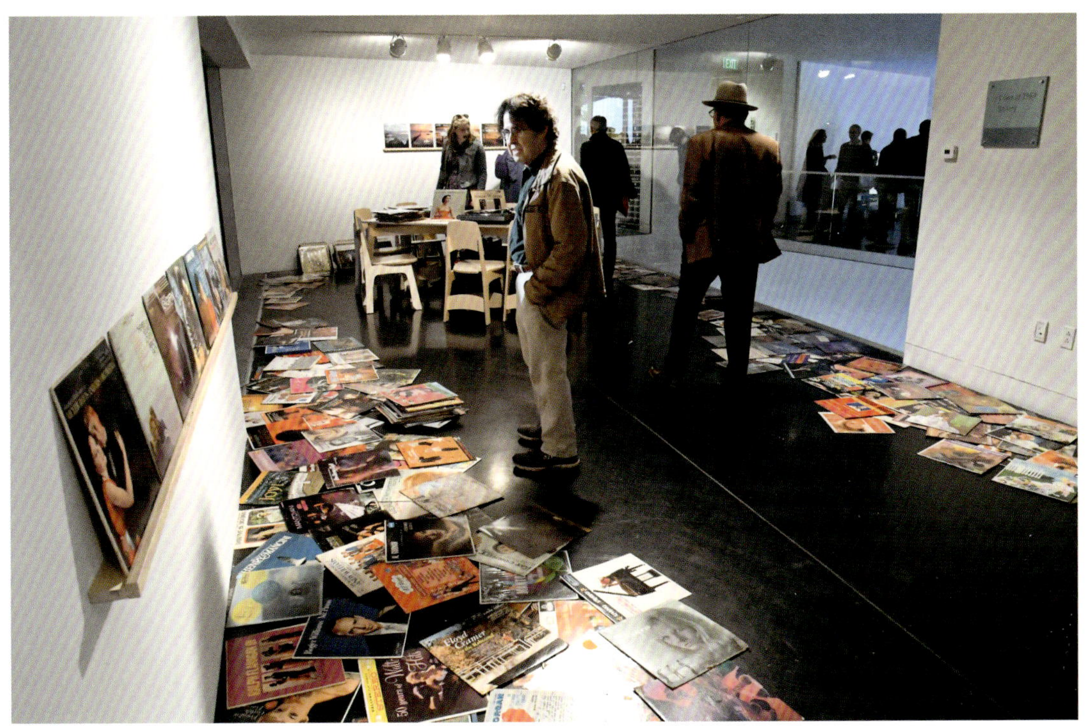

(above and facing)

Uneasy Listening, 2018
Mixed media
Dimensions variable
Installation view, Tang Museum, Saratoga Springs, New York, 2018

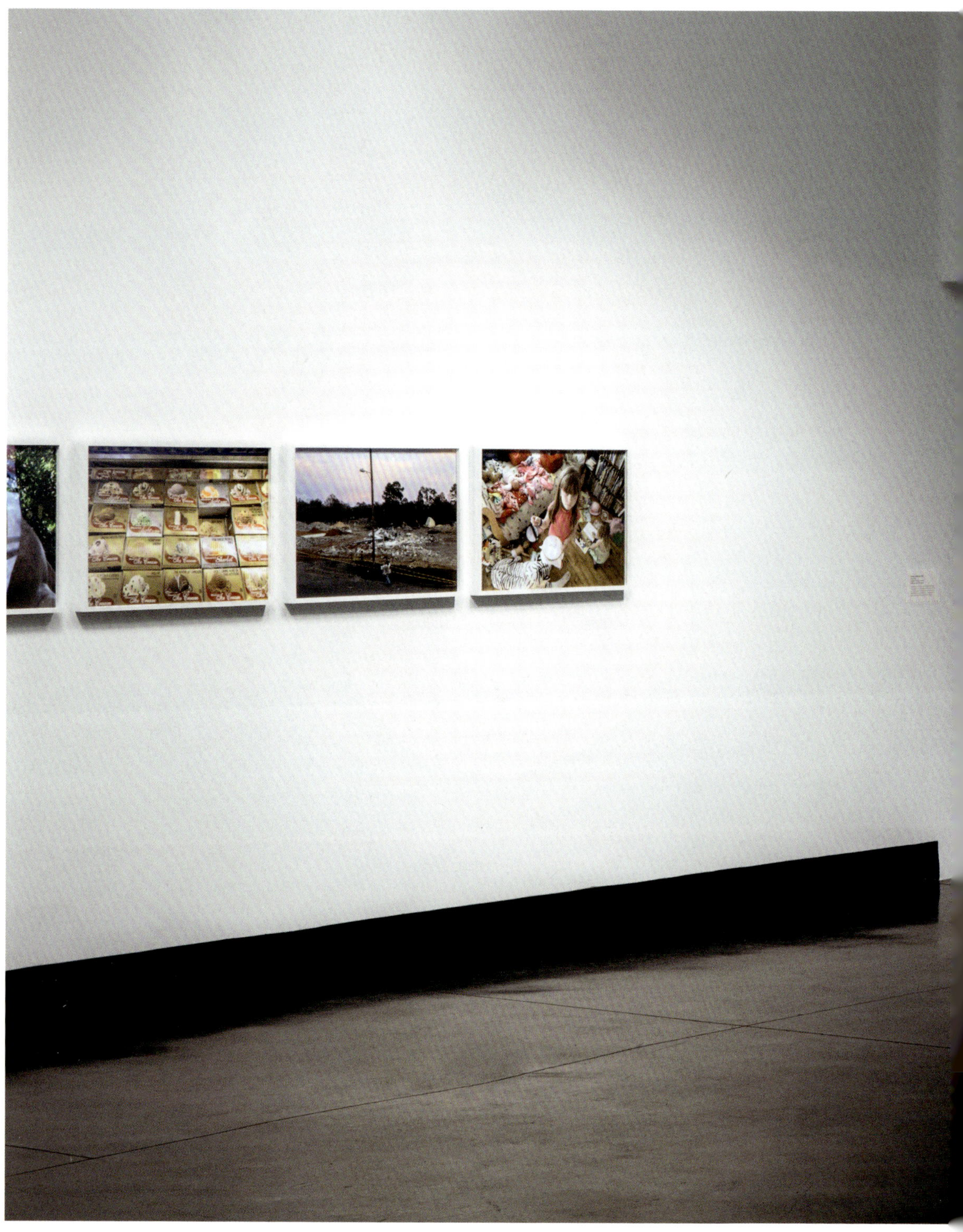

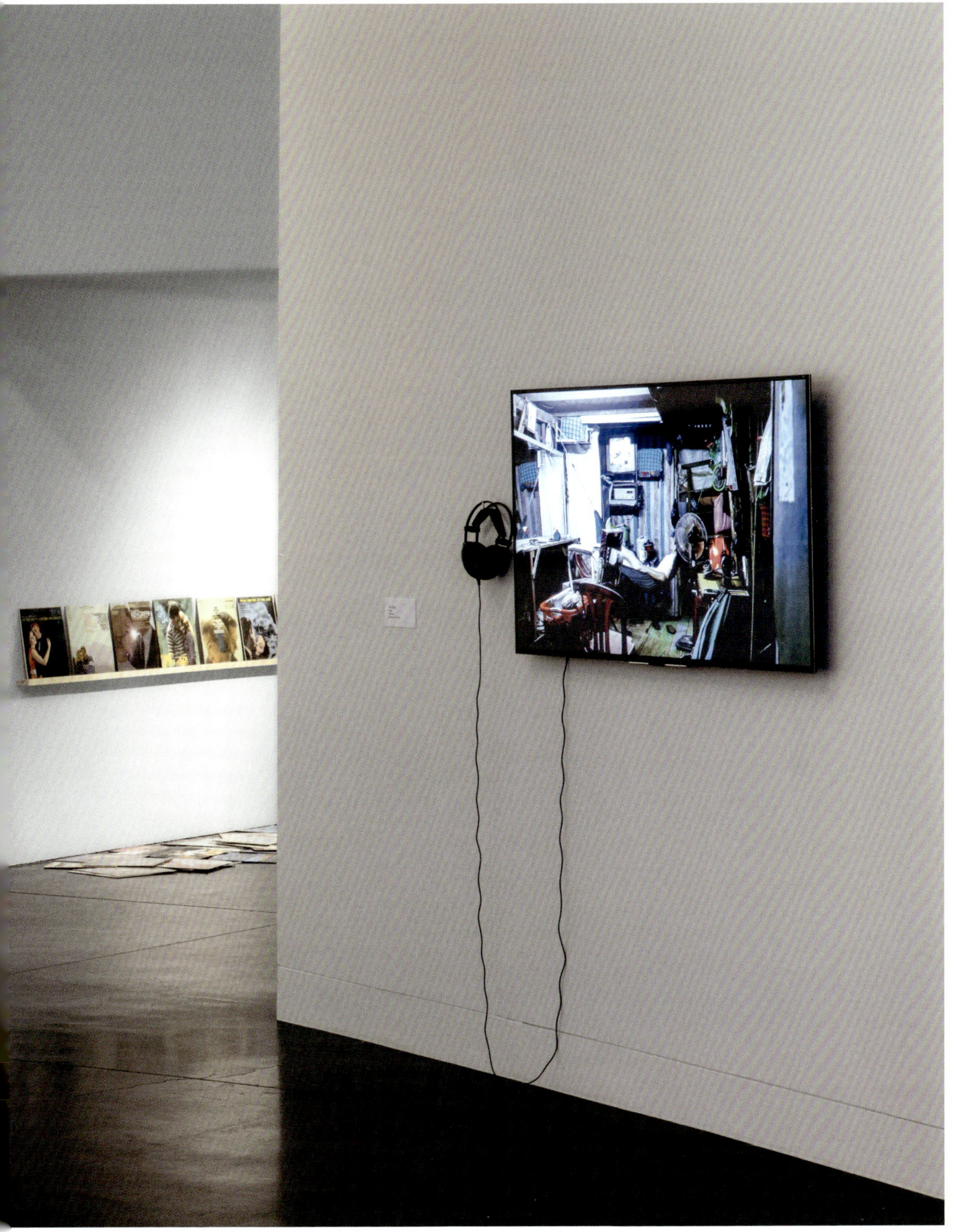

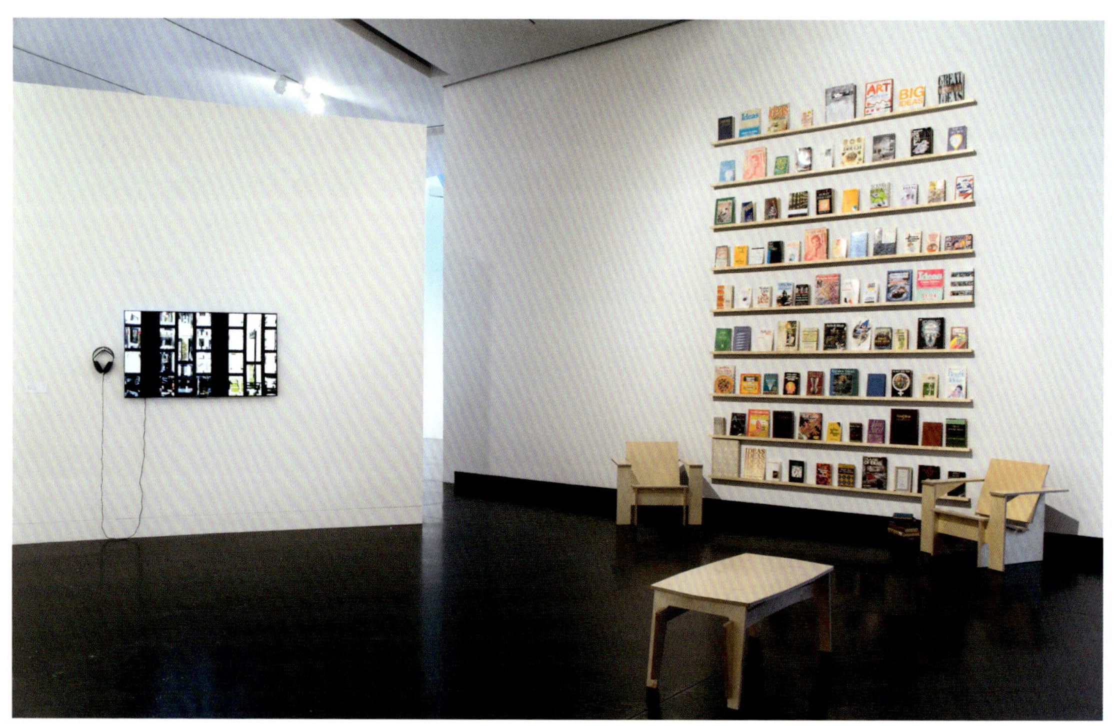

(previous spread)

Installation view with *VTV*, 2011, video, 21 minutes, Tang Museum, Saratoga Springs, New York, 2018

(above and facing)

Installation views with *VTV*, 2011, video, 21 minutes, and *Library of Ideas*, 2018, mixed media, dimensions variable, Tang Museum, Saratoga Springs, New York, 2018

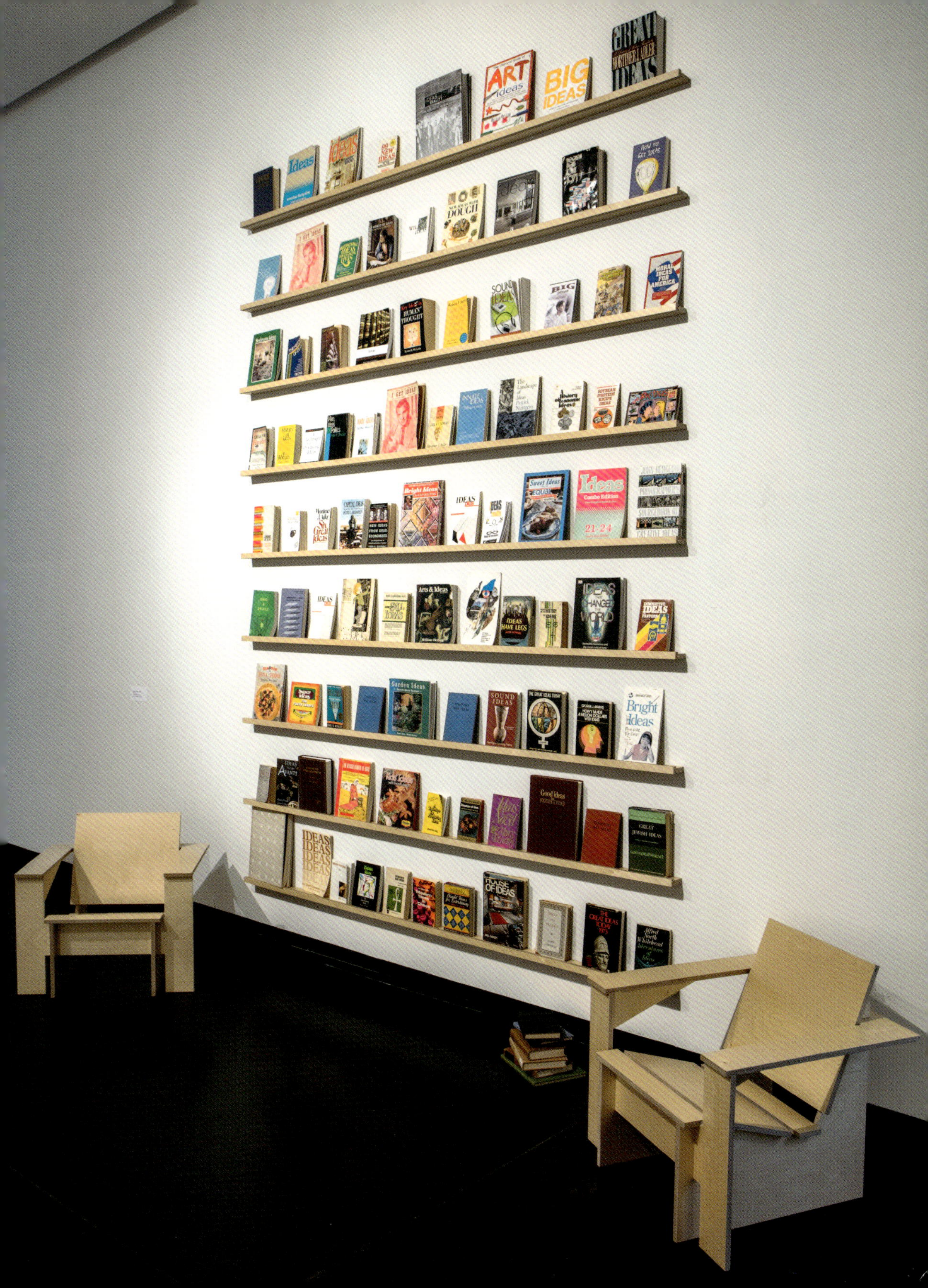
GREAT IDEAS
MORTIMER J. ADLER
ART ideas
BIG IDEAS
Ideas
HUMAN THOUGHT
MORAL IDEAS FOR AMERICA
Bright Ideas
Ideas
Combo Edition
Arts & Ideas
IDEAS HAVE LEGS
SOUND IDEAS
Garden Ideas
Good Ideas
GREAT JEWISH IDEAS
IDEAS IDEAS IDEAS IDEAS
HOUSE OF IDEAS
THE GREAT IDEAS TODAY 1973

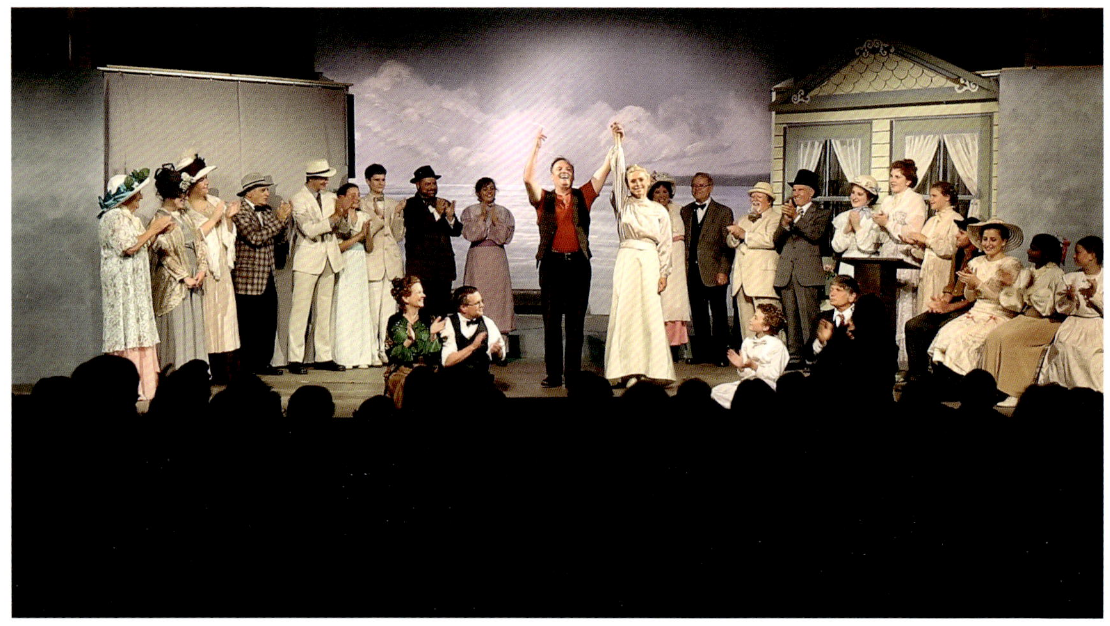

(above and facing)

Curtain Calls, 2018
(video stills)
Video
11 minutes

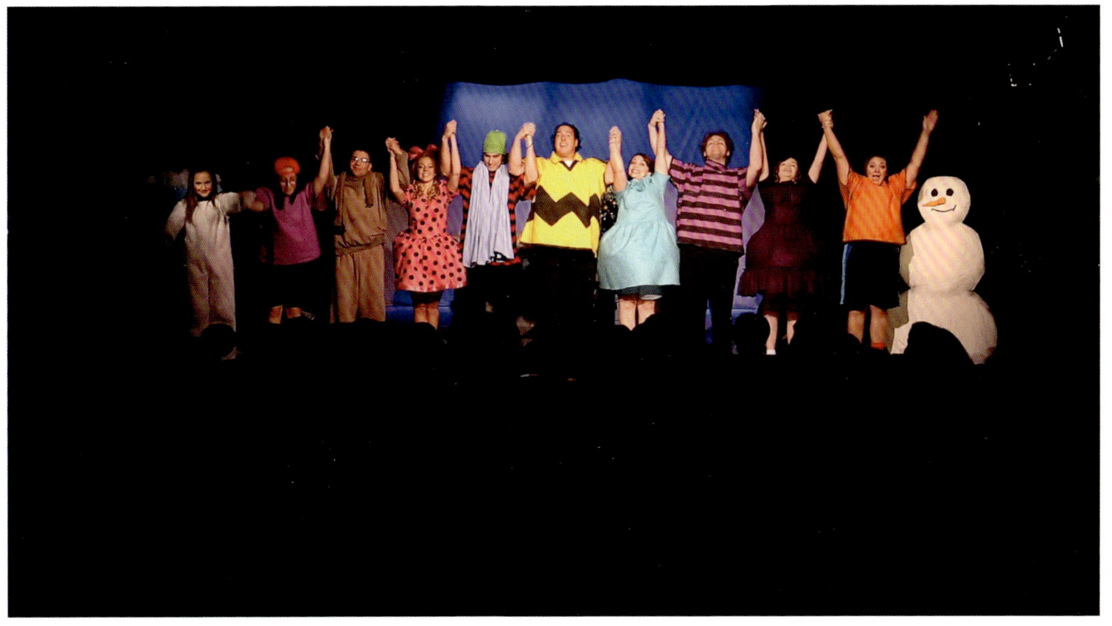

(following spread)

Installation view with *Cartoons*, 2018, 16 archival inkjet prints, 24 x 30 inches each, and *Tunisian Radios*, 2008–2018, video, 12 minutes 20 seconds, Tang Museum, Saratoga Springs, New York, 2018

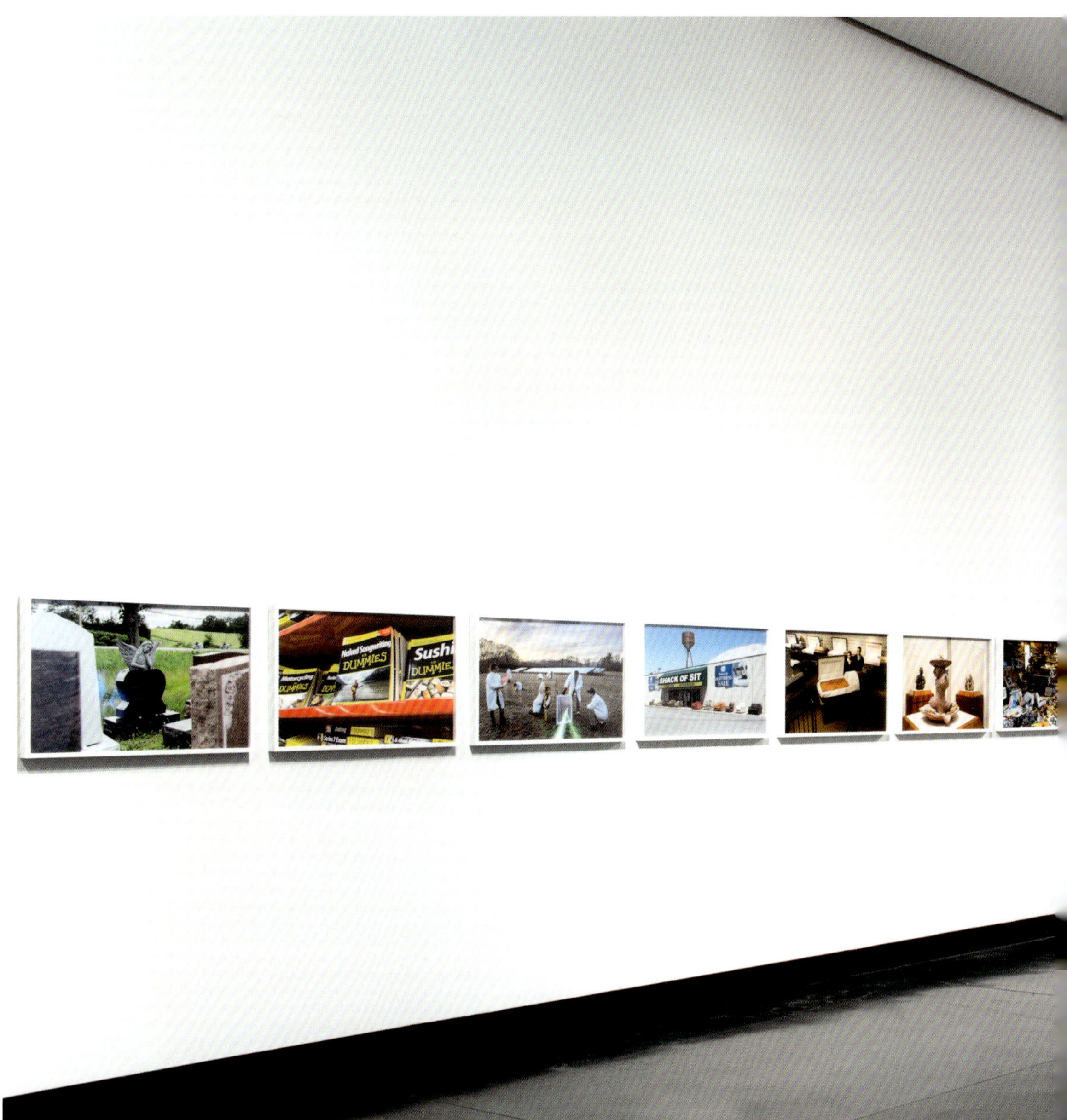
Naked Songwriting
DUMMIES
Sushi
DUMMIES
Motorcycling
DUMMIES
SHACK OF SIT

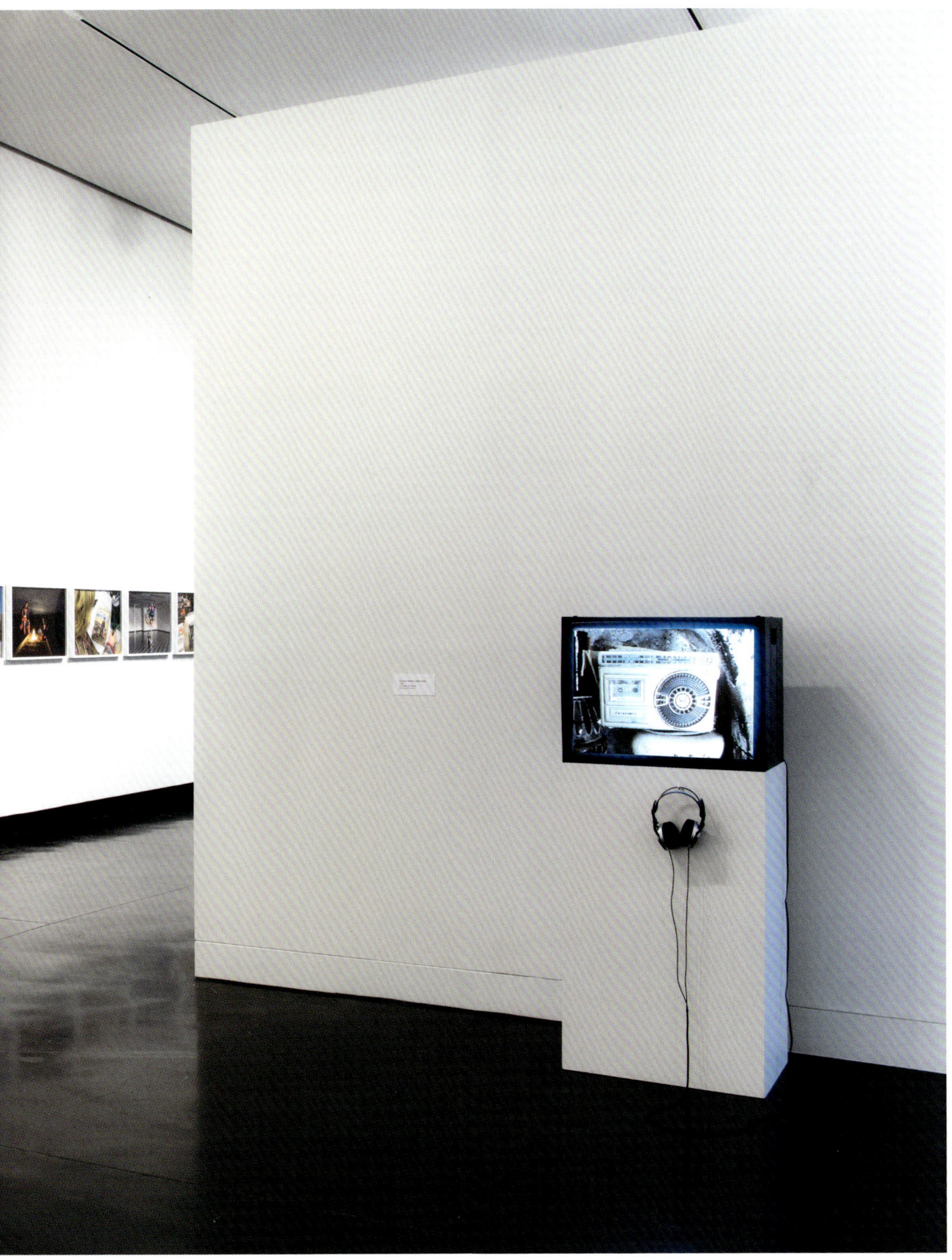

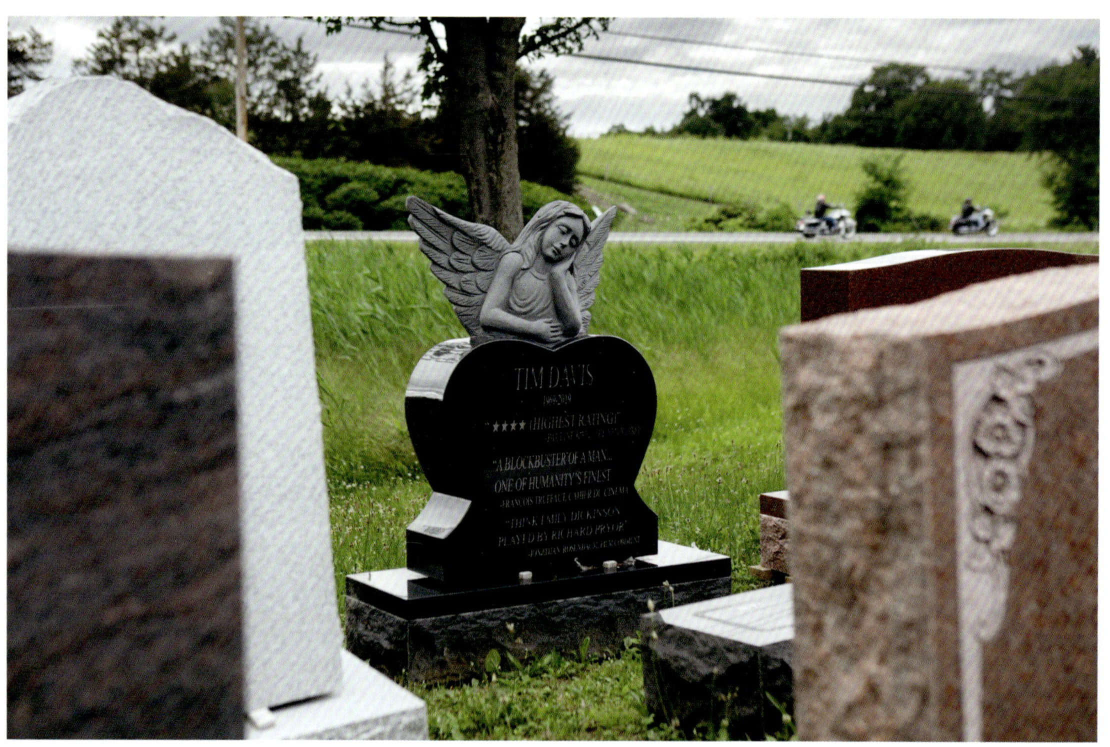

My Gravestone from
Cartoons, 2018
Archival inkjet print
24 x 30 inches

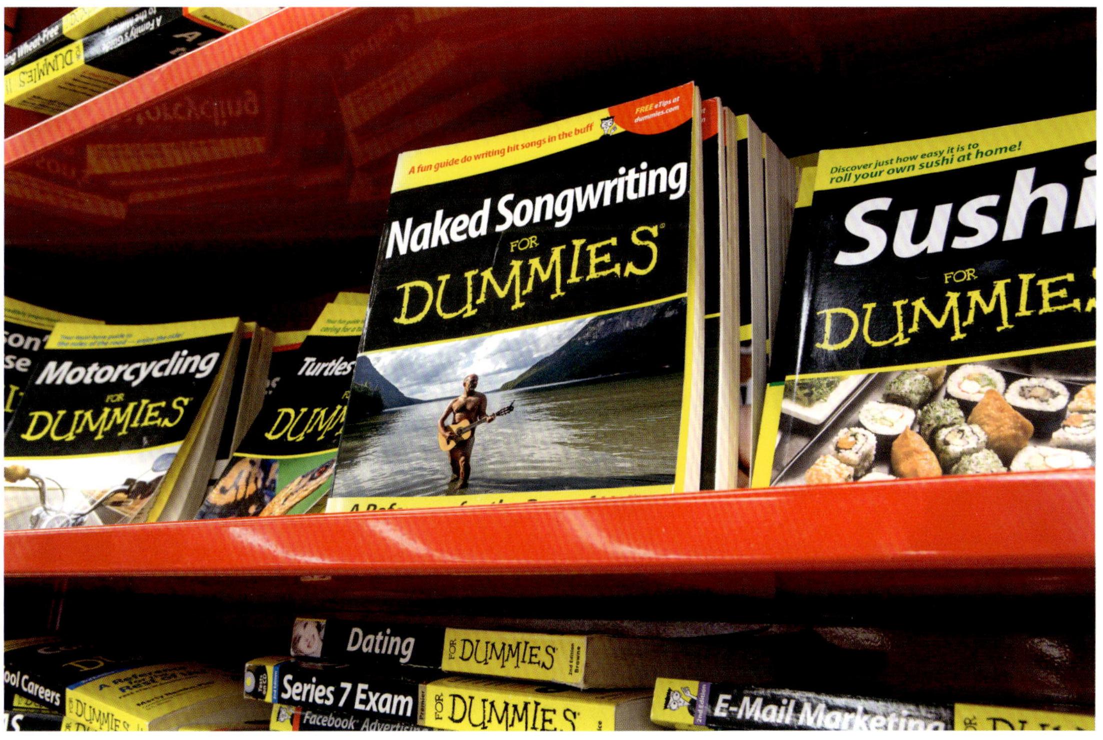

Naked Songwriting for Dummies from *Cartoons*,
2018
Archival inkjet print
24 x 30 inches

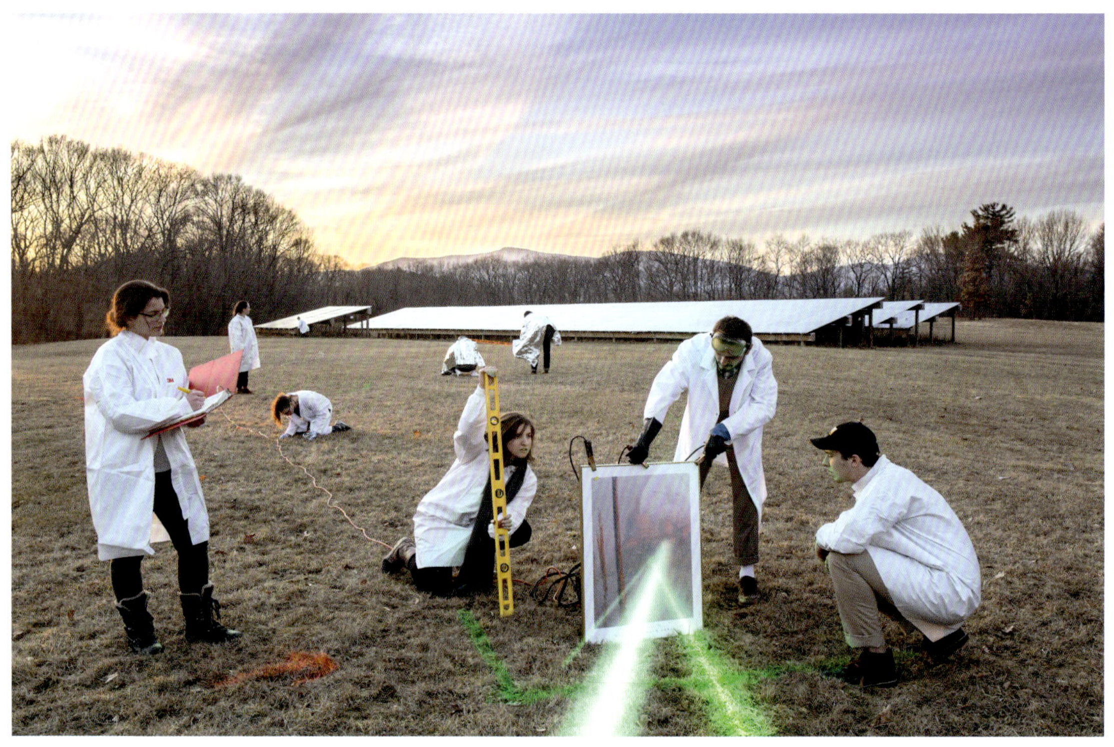

The First Solar-Powered Monet Poster
from *Cartoons*, 2018
Archival inkjet print
24 x 30 inches

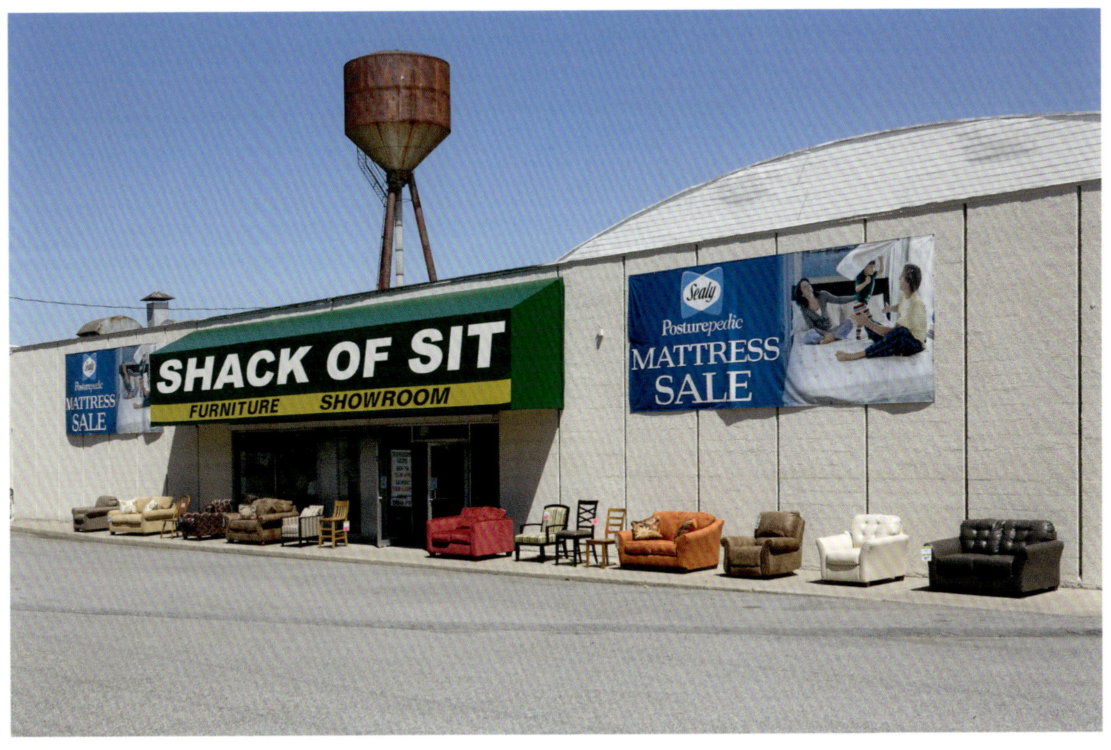

Shack of Sit
from *Cartoons*, 2018
Archival inkjet print
24 x 30 inches

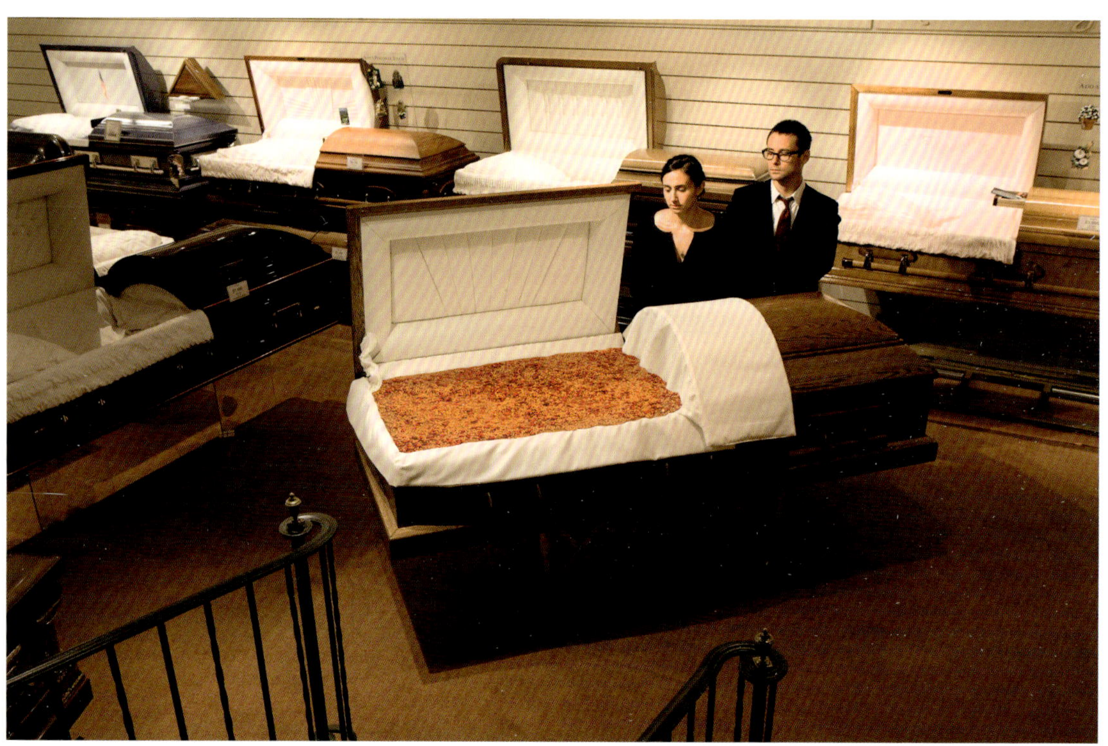

Coffin Full of Beans
from *Cartoons*, 2018
Archival inkjet print
24 x 30 inches

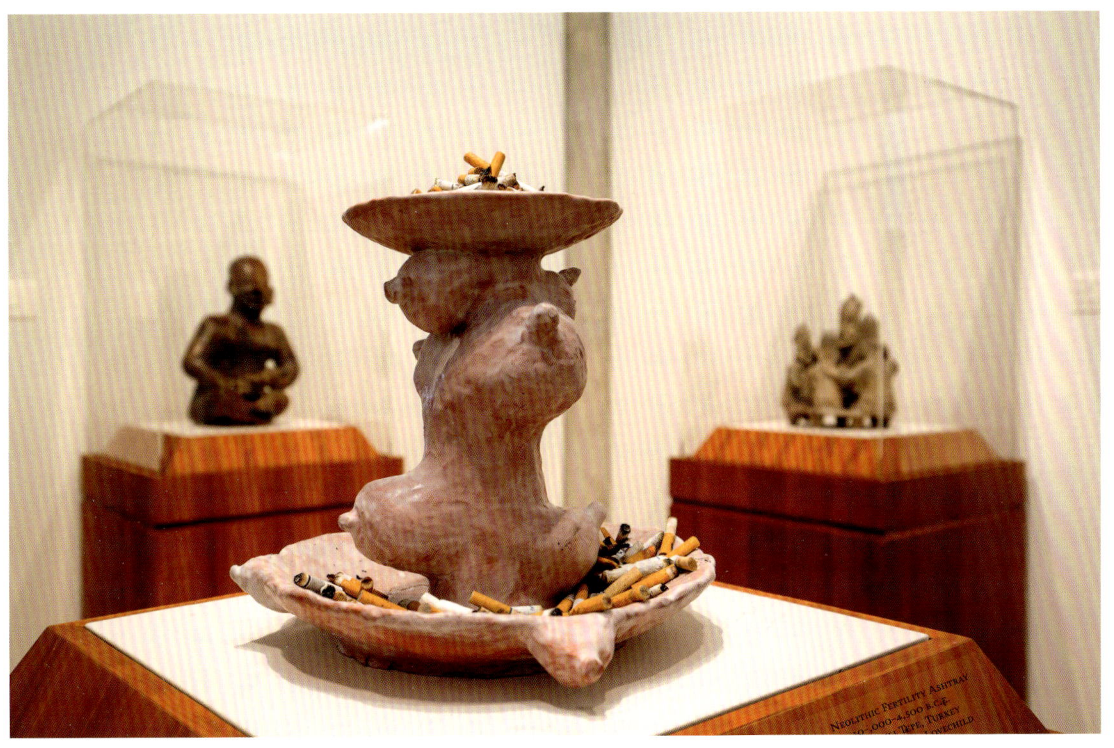

Neolithic Fertility Ashtray
from *Cartoons*, 2018
Archival inkjet print
24 x 30 inches

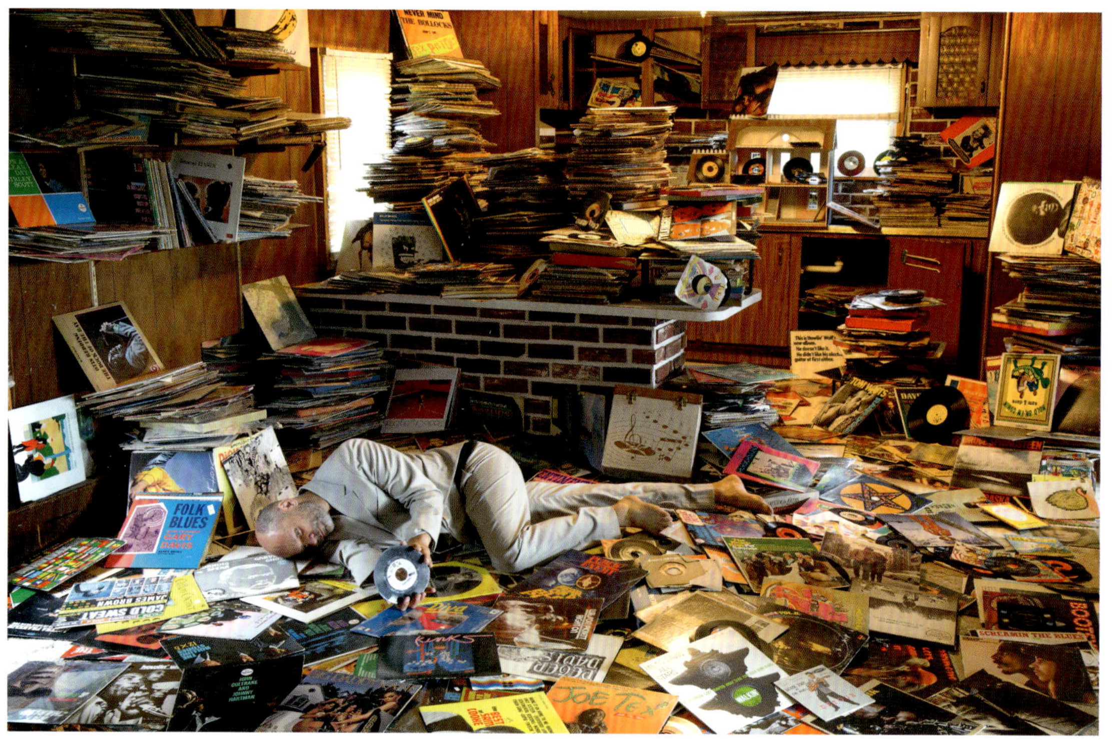

The Collector
from *Cartoons*, 2018
Archival inkjet print
24 x 30 inches

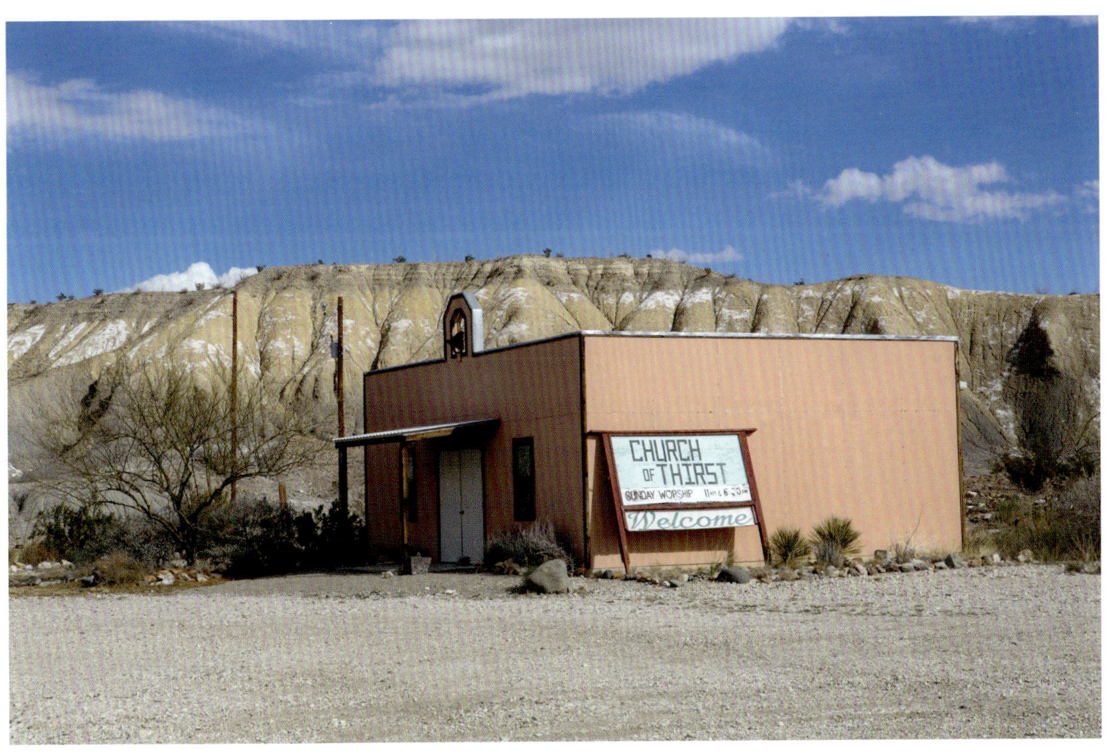

Church of Thirst
from *Cartoons*, 2018
Archival inkjet print
24 x 30 inches

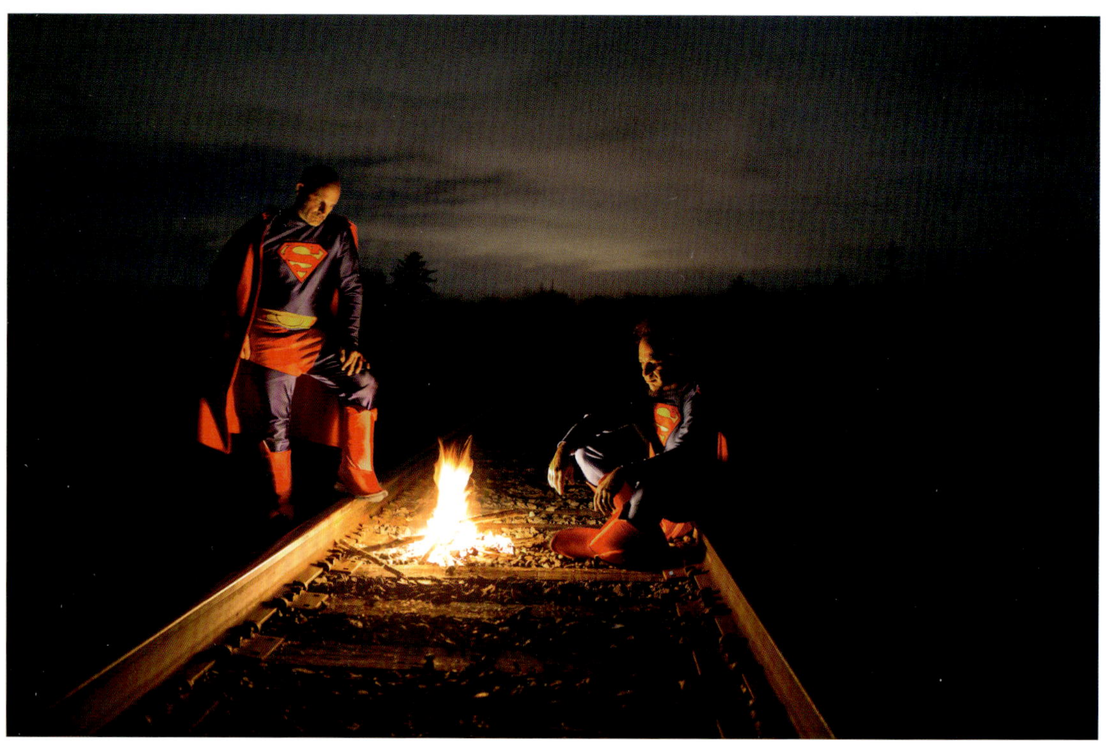

Hobo Supermen
from *Cartoons*, 2018
Archival inkjet print
24 x 30 inches

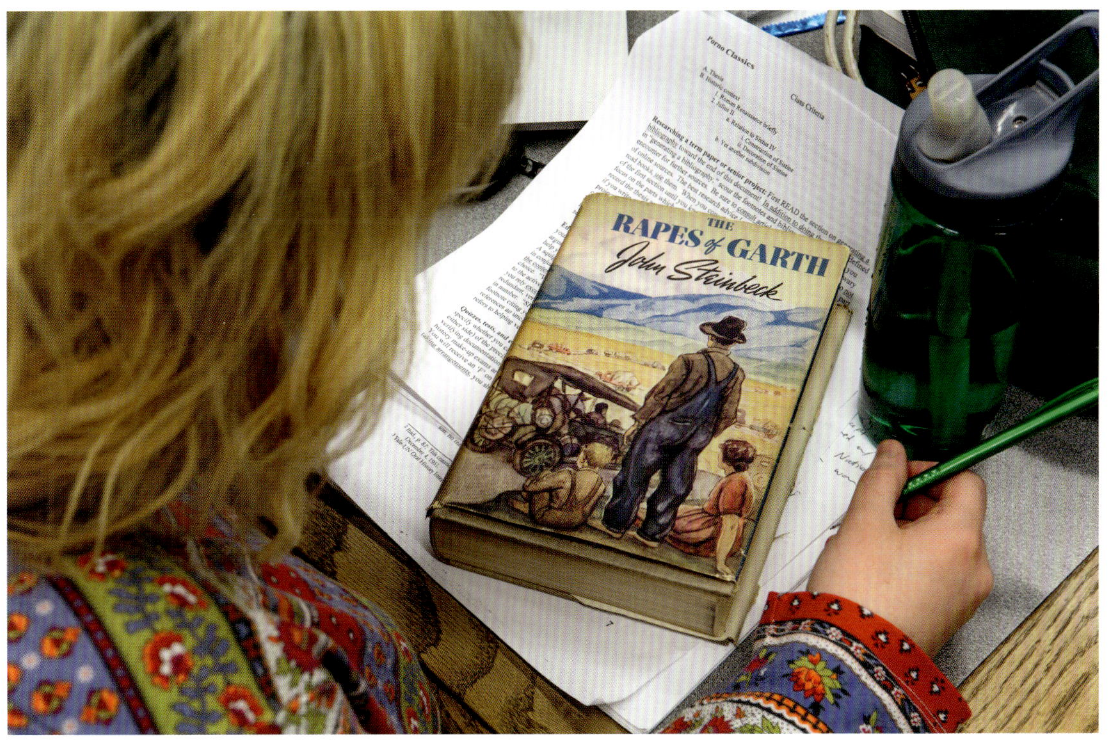

Porno Classics
from *Cartoons*, 2018
Archival inkjet print
24 x 30 inches

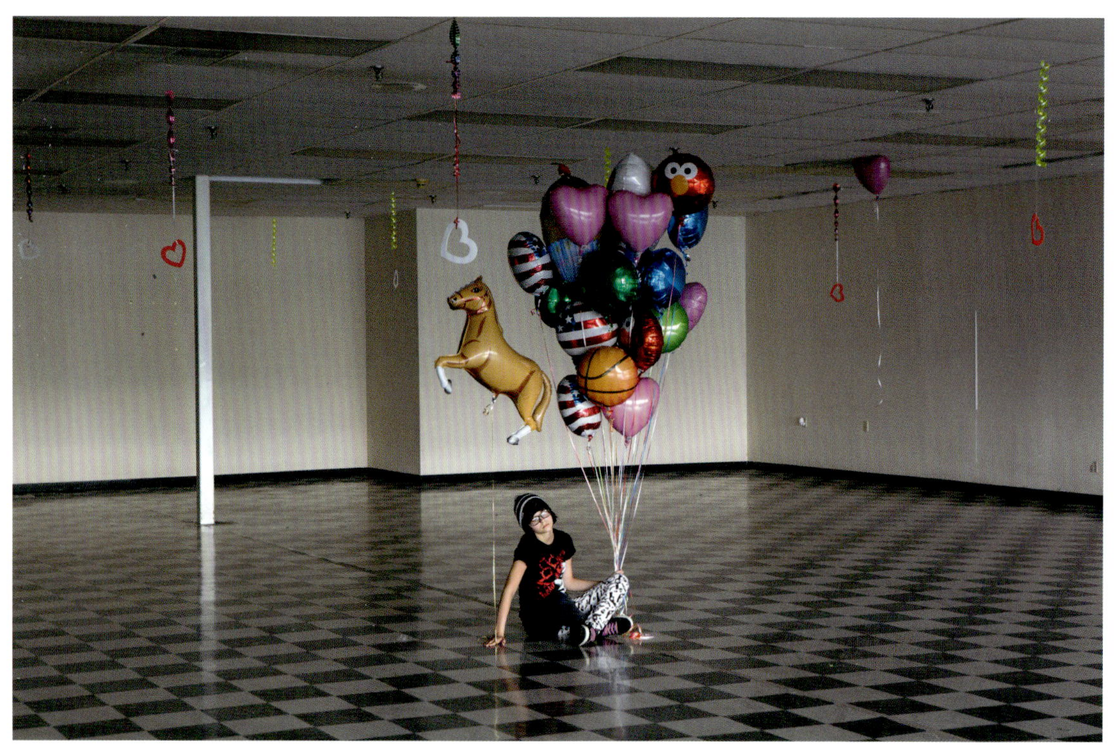

Sad Balloons
from *Cartoons*, 2018
Archival inkjet print
24 x 30 inches

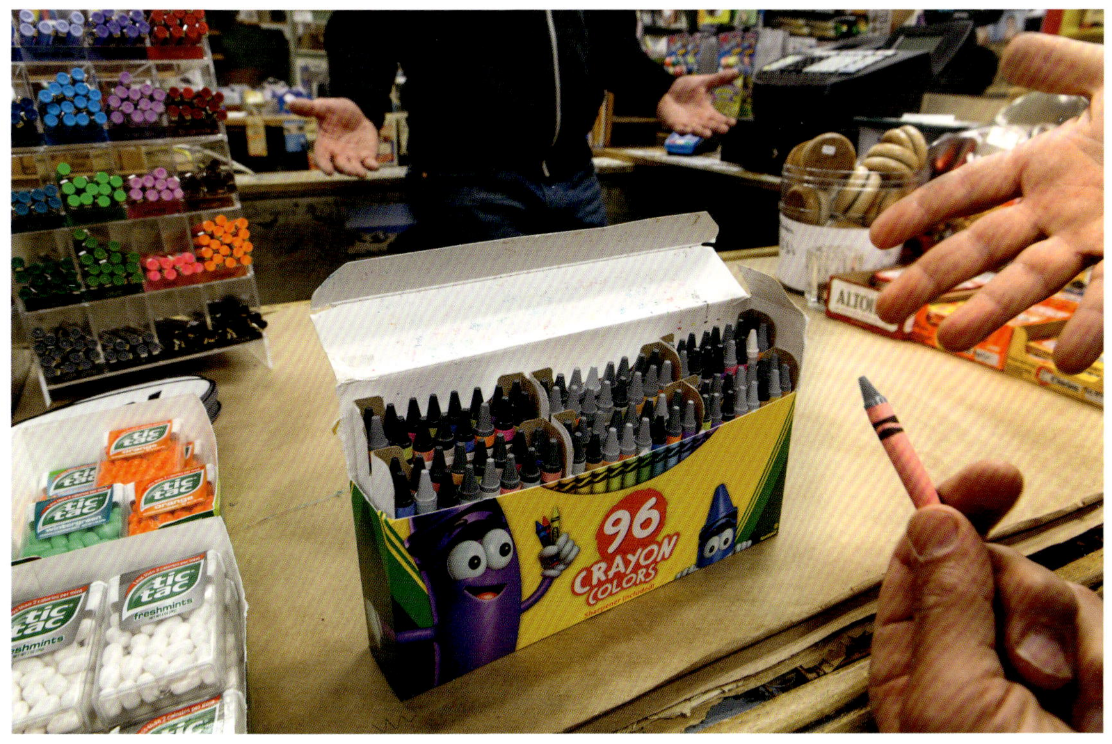

Gray Crayons
from *Cartoons*, 2018
Archival inkjet print
24 x 30 inches

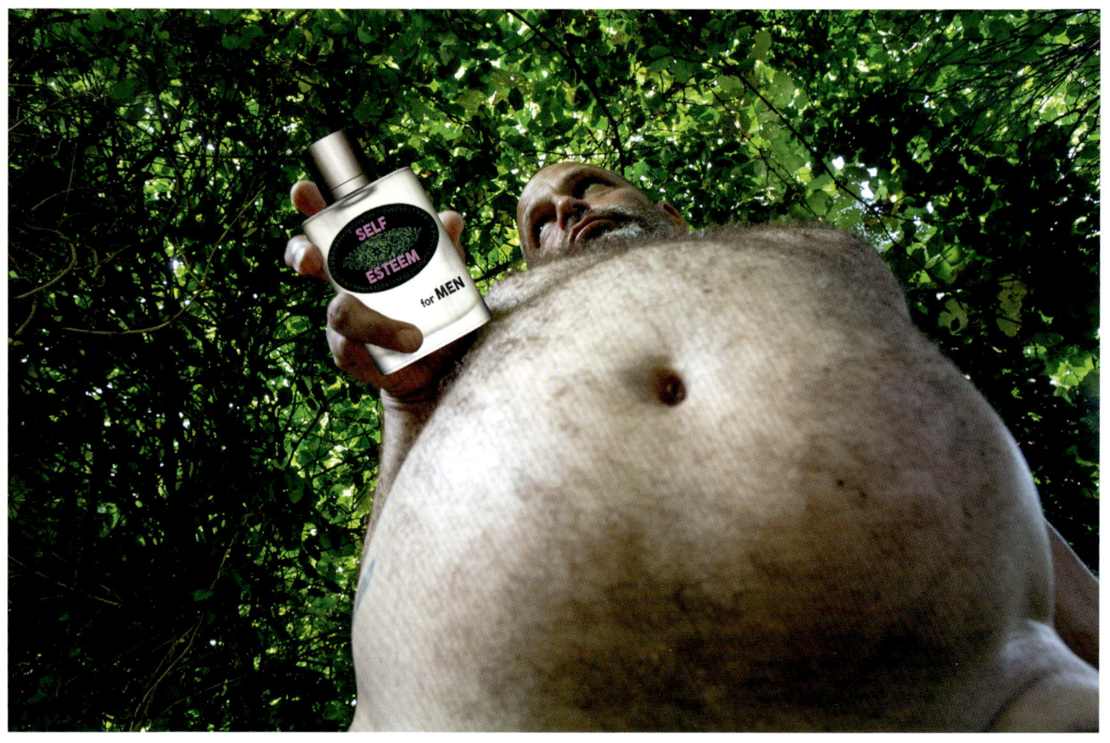

Self Esteem for Men
from *Cartoons*, 2018
Archival inkjet print
24 x 30 inches

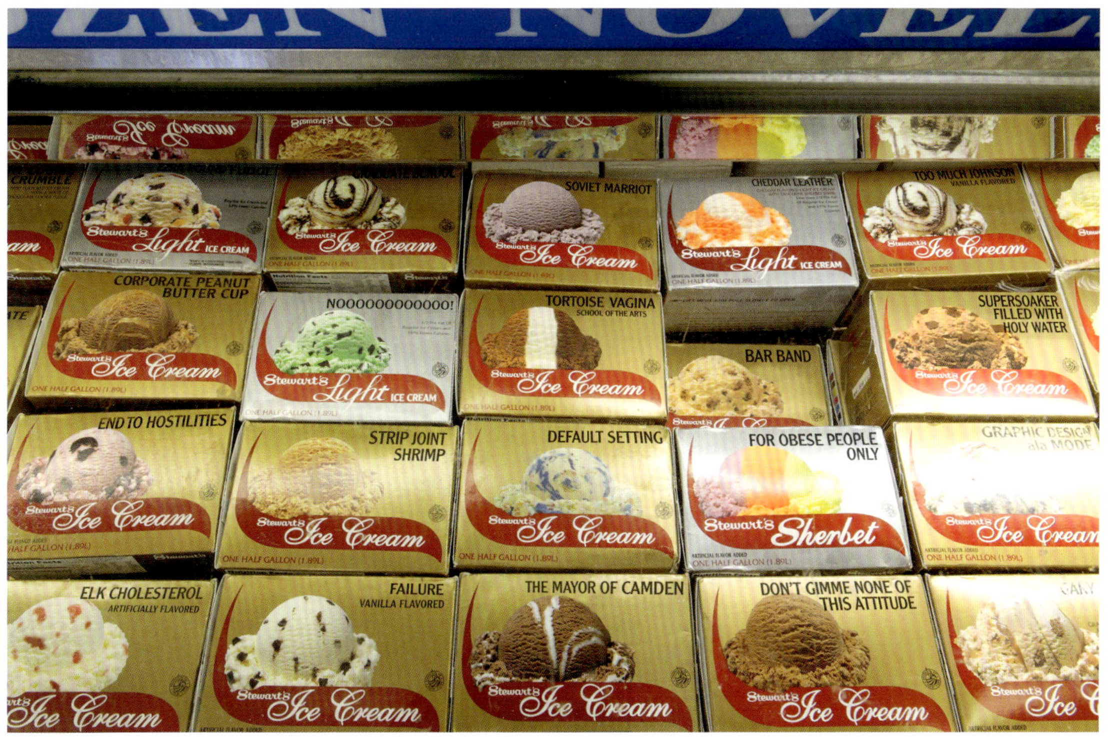

Ice Cream Flavors
from *Cartoons*, 2018
Archival inkjet print
24 x 30 inches

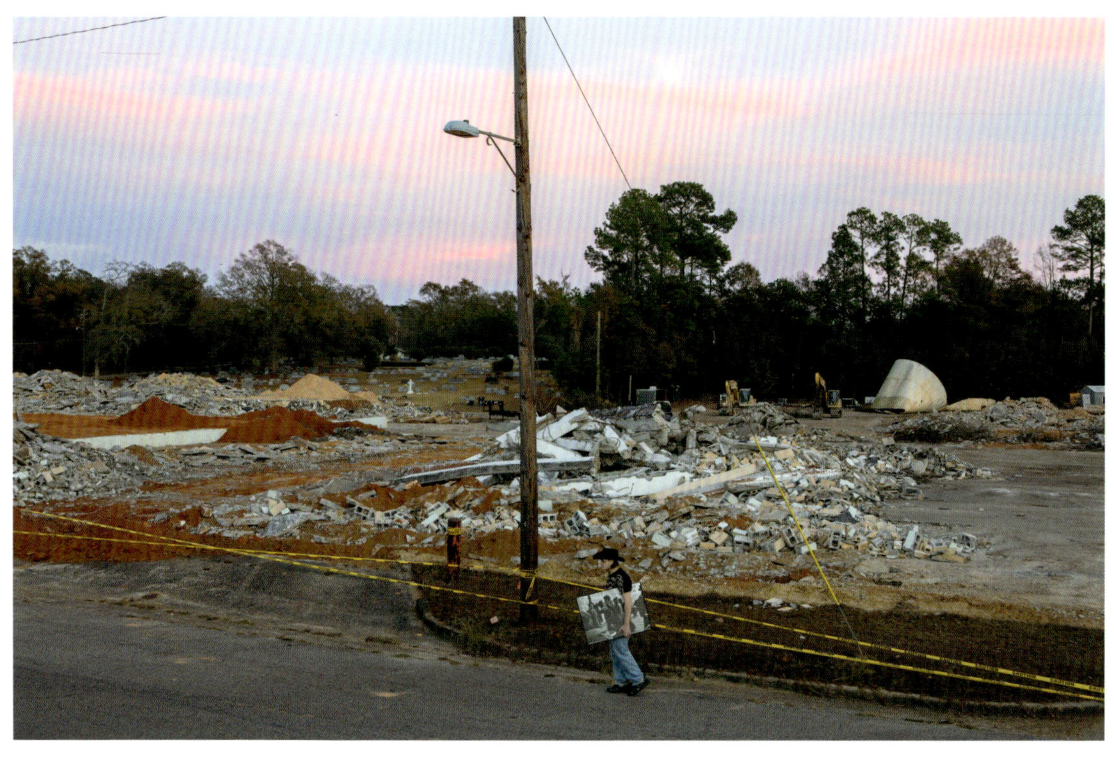

Art History
from *Cartoons*, 2018
Archival inkjet print
24 x 30 inches

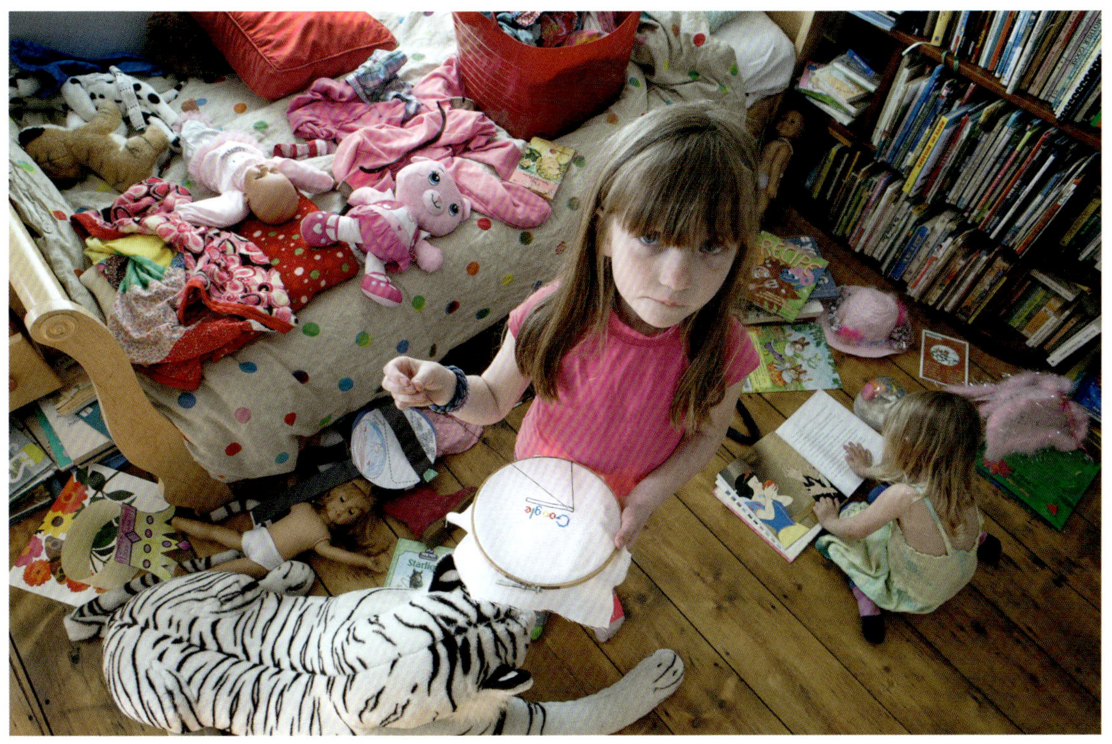

Google Cross Stitch
from *Cartoons*, 2018
Archival inkjet print
24 x 30 inches

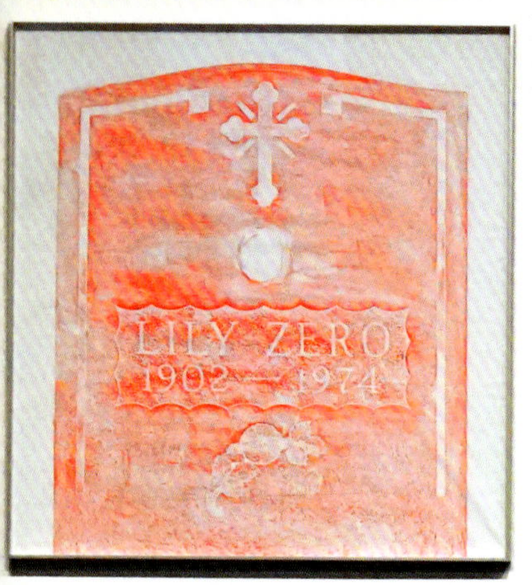
LILY ZERO
1902 — 1974

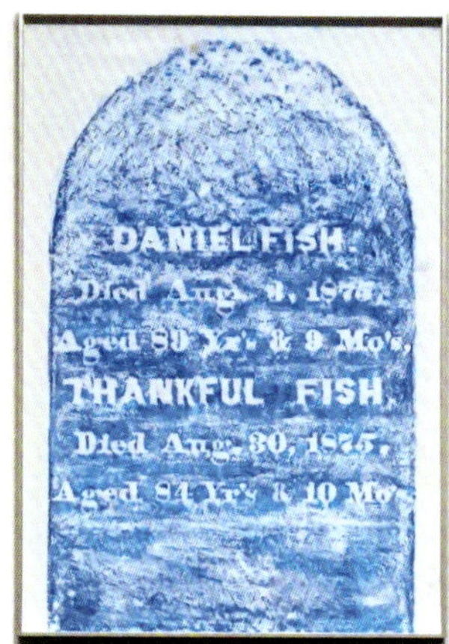
DANIEL FISH
THANKFUL FISH

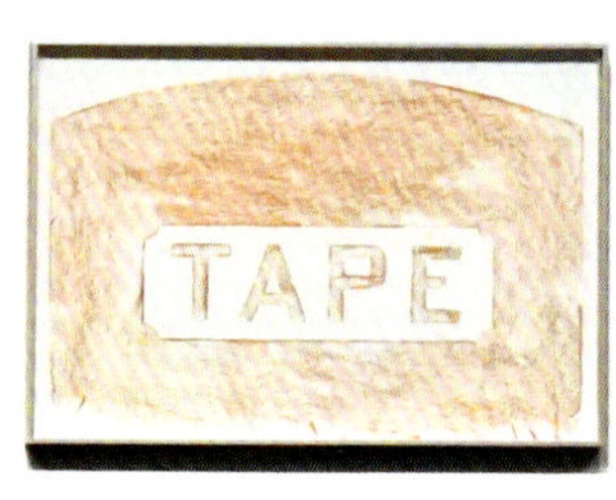
TAPE

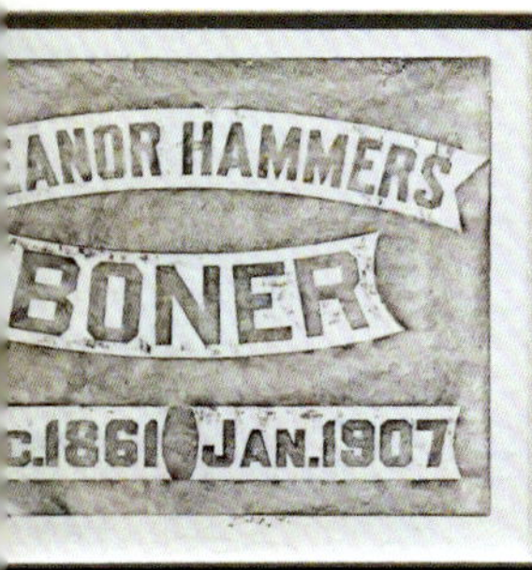
ANOR HAMMERS
BONER
C.1861 JAN.1907

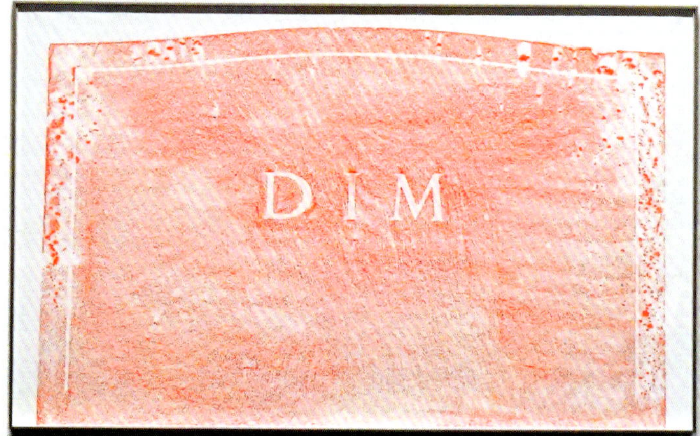
DIM

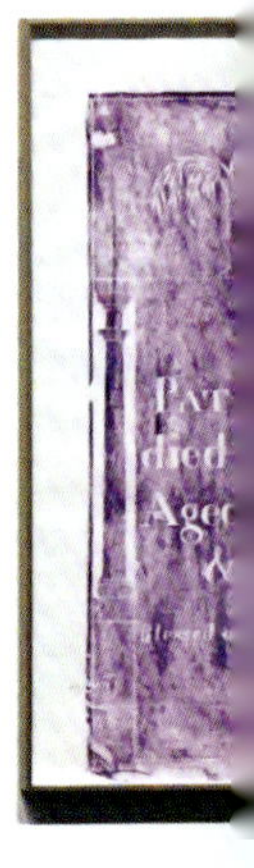

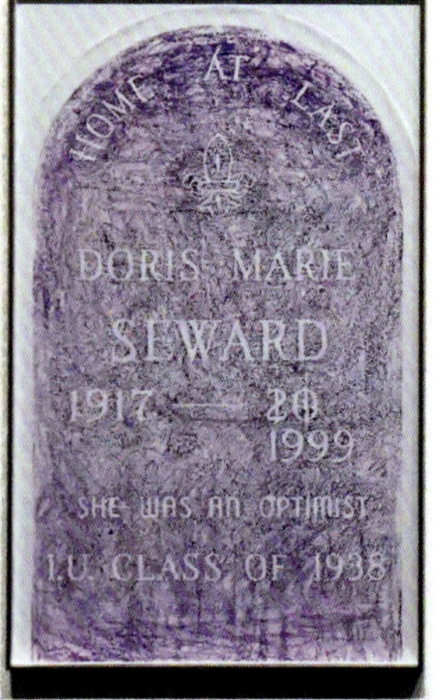
HOME AT LAST
DORIS MARIE
SEWARD
1917 — 20
1999
SHE WAS AN OPTIMIST
I.U. CLASS OF 1938

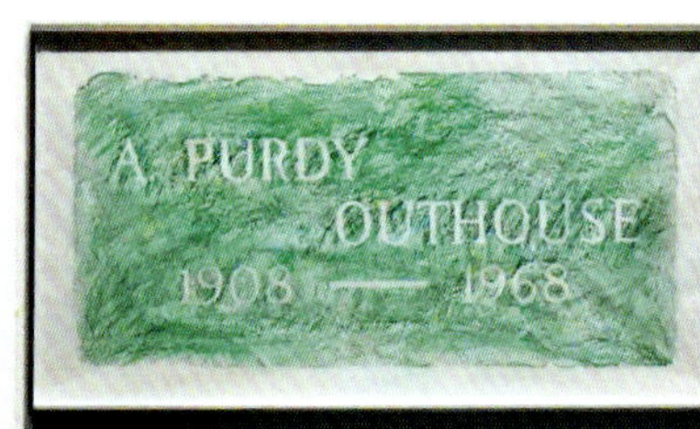
A. PURDY
OUTHOUSE
1908 — 1968

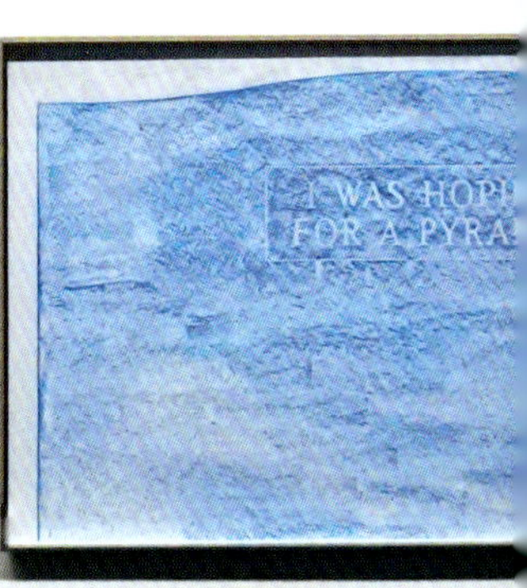
I WAS HOP
FOR A PYRA

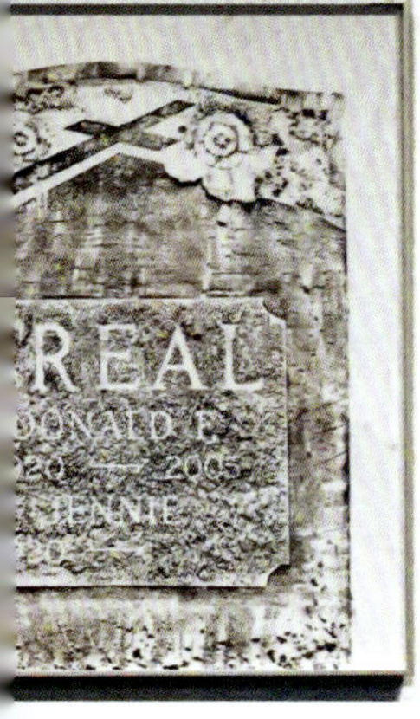
REAL

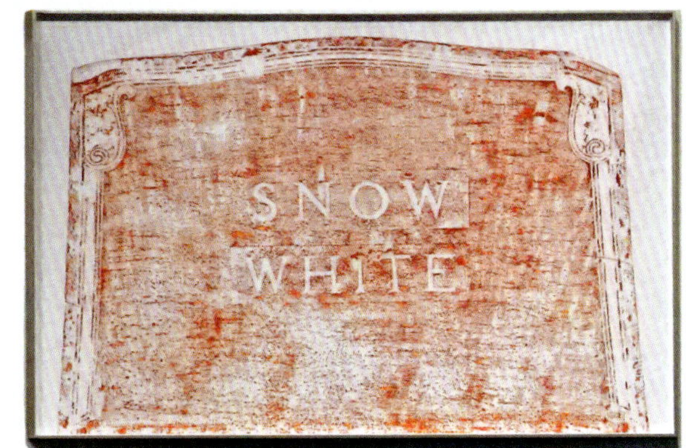
SNOW
WHITE

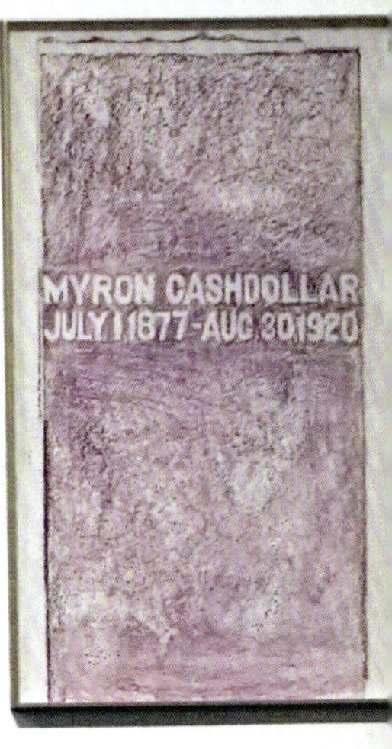
MYRON CASHDOLLAR
JULY 1 1877-AUG 30 1920

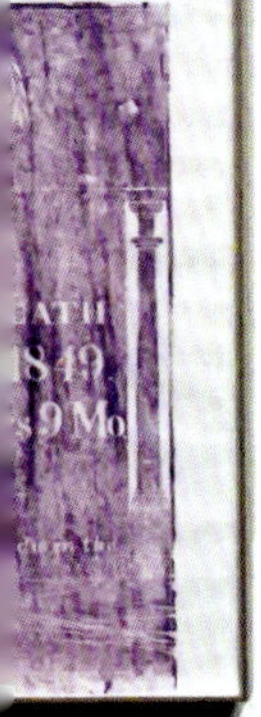

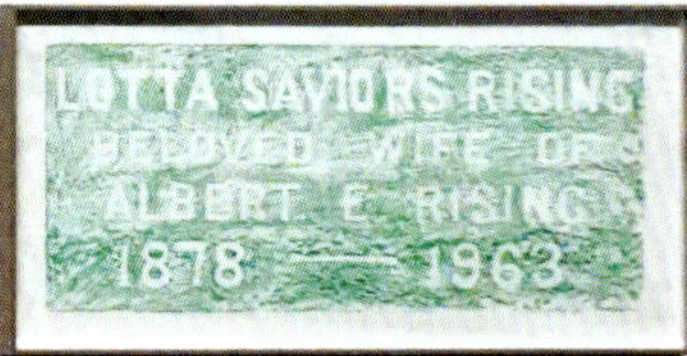
LOTTA SAVIORS RISING
BELOVED WIFE OF
ALBERT E. RISING
1878 — 1963

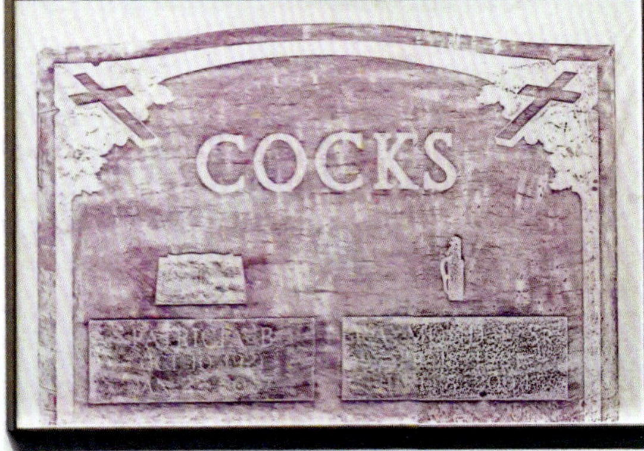
COCKS

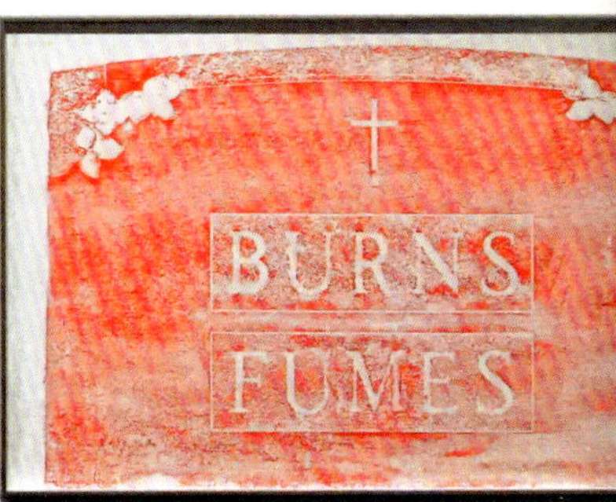
BURNS
FUMES

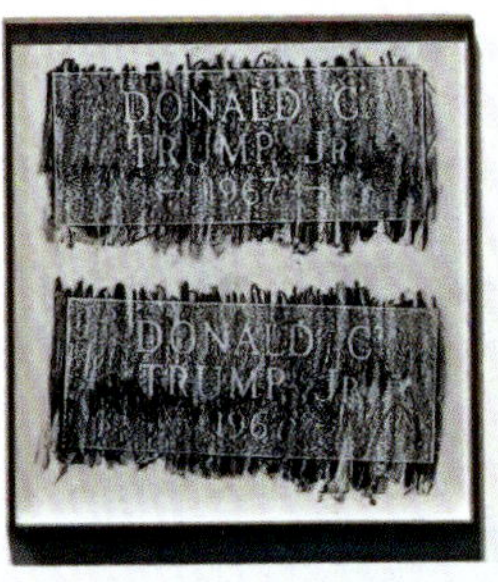
DONALD C.
TRUMP JR.
DONALD C.
TRUMP JR.

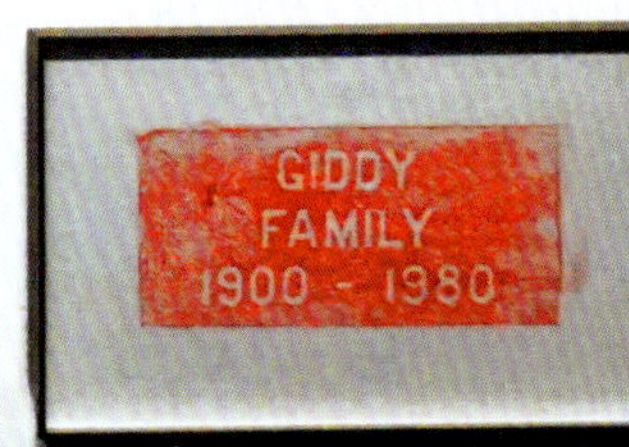
GIDDY
FAMILY
1900 - 1980

(previous spread)

Light Comedy Grave Rubbings, 2018
17 works, crayon on paper
Dimensions variable
Installation view, Tang Museum, Saratoga Springs, New York, 2018

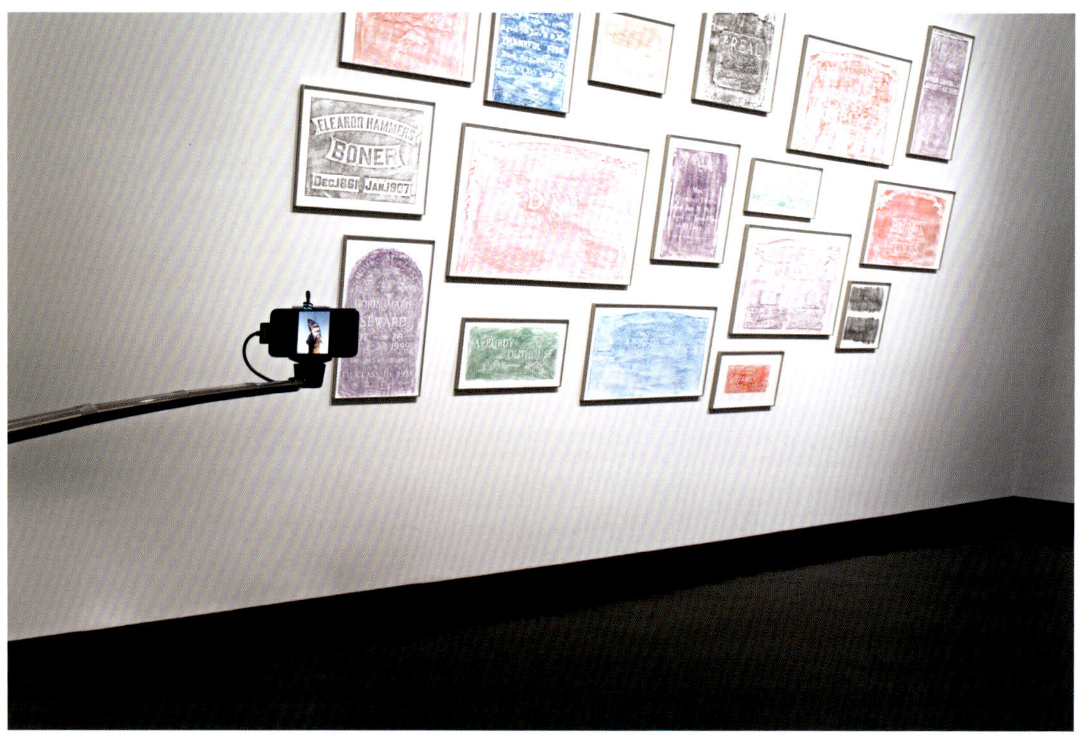

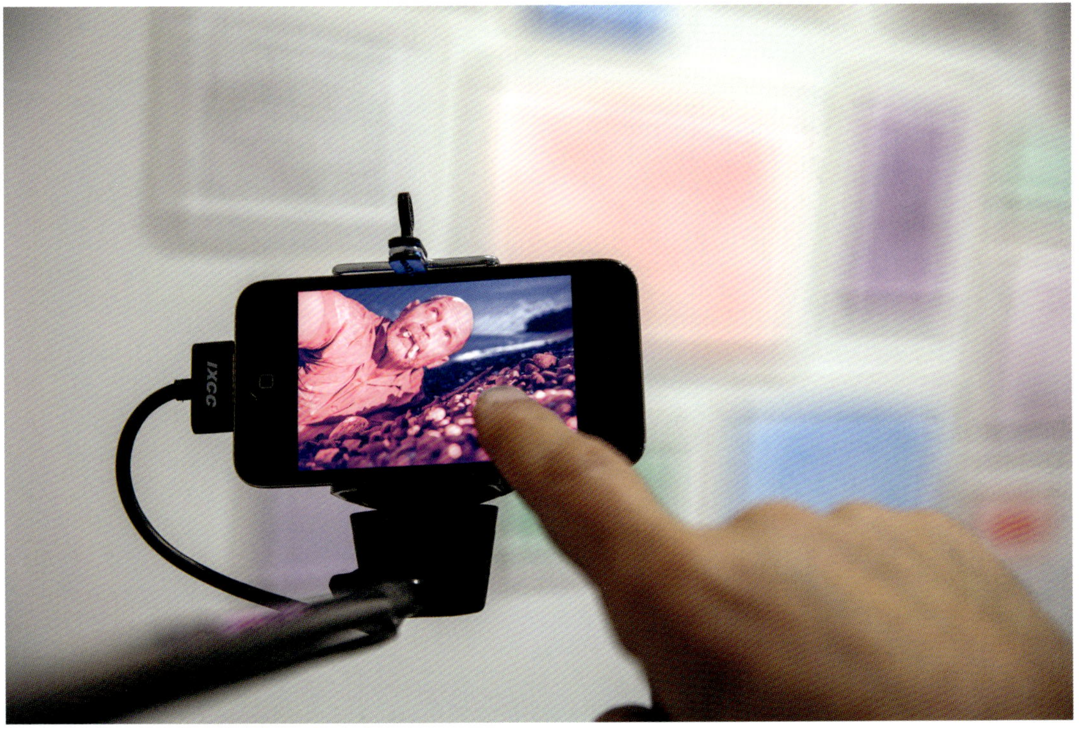

(above and facing, details on following spread)

South Sea Selfies, 2017
Digital photographs,
iPod, selfie stick
Dimensions variable
Installation views,
Tang Museum, Saratoga
Springs, New York, 2018

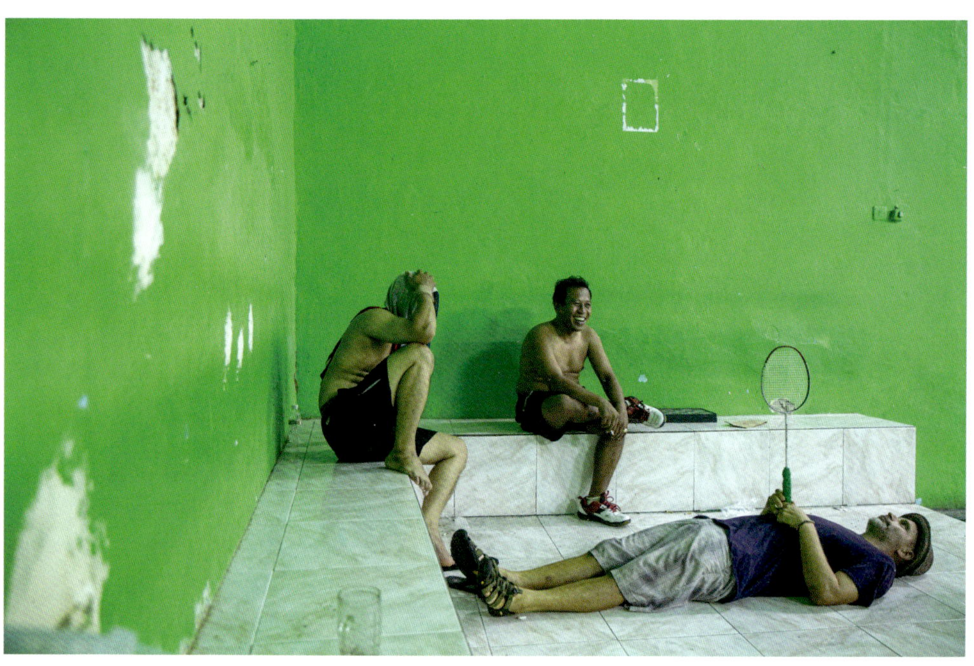

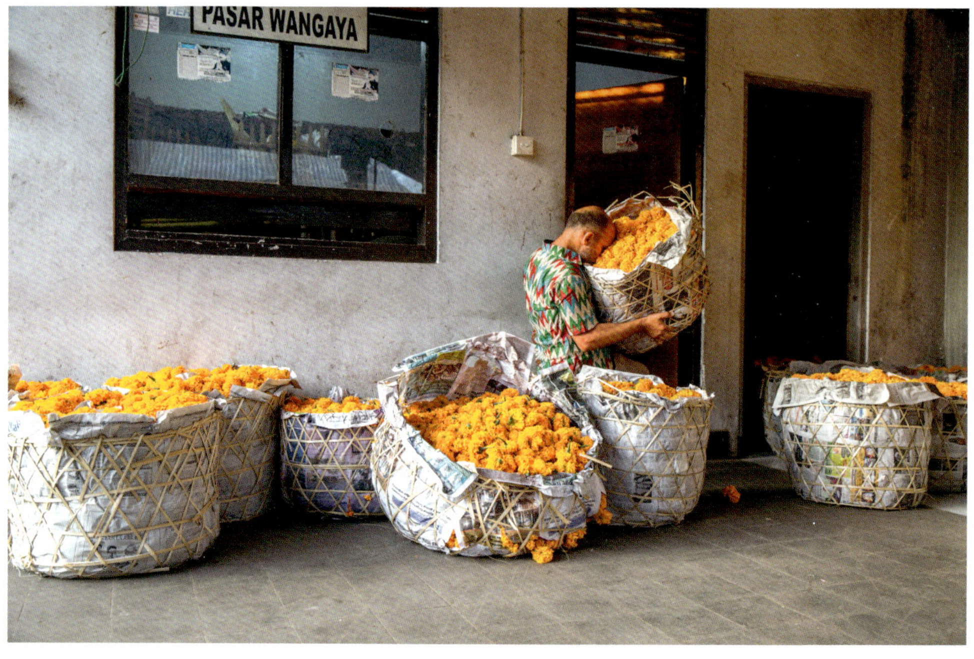
PASAR WANGAYA

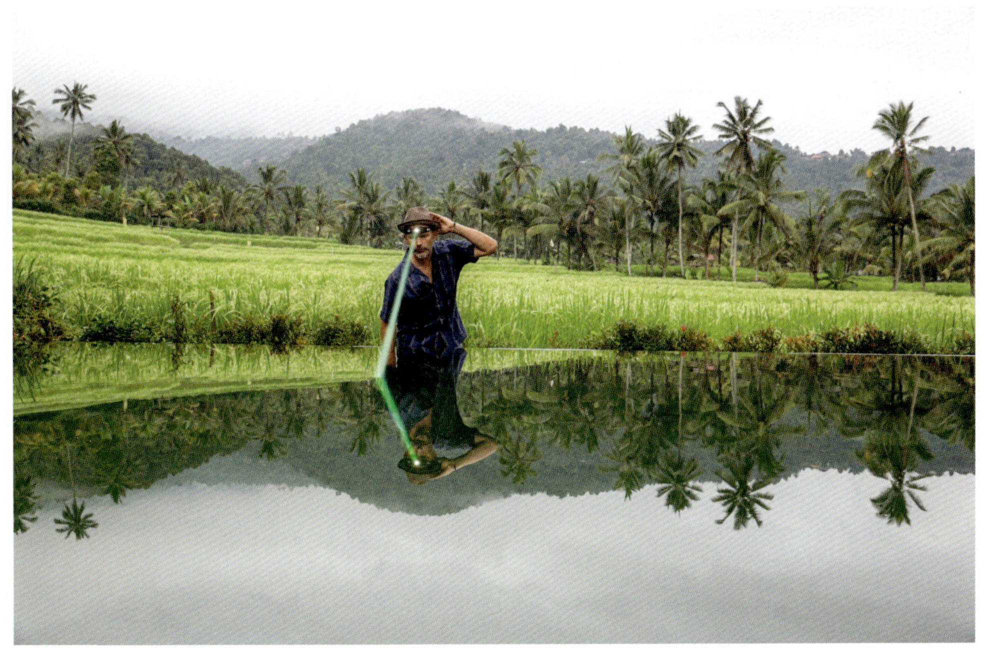

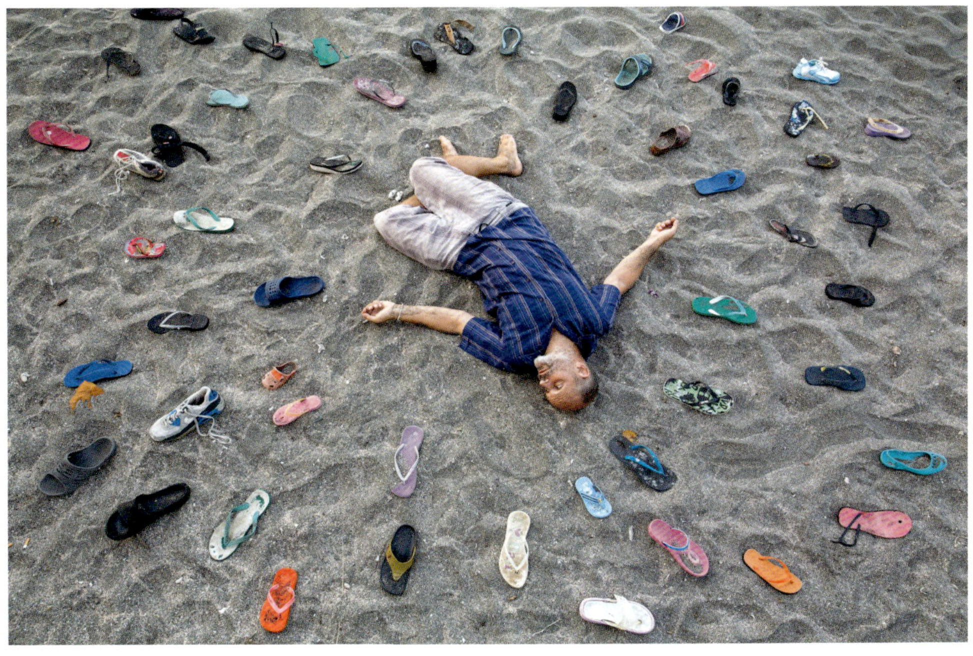

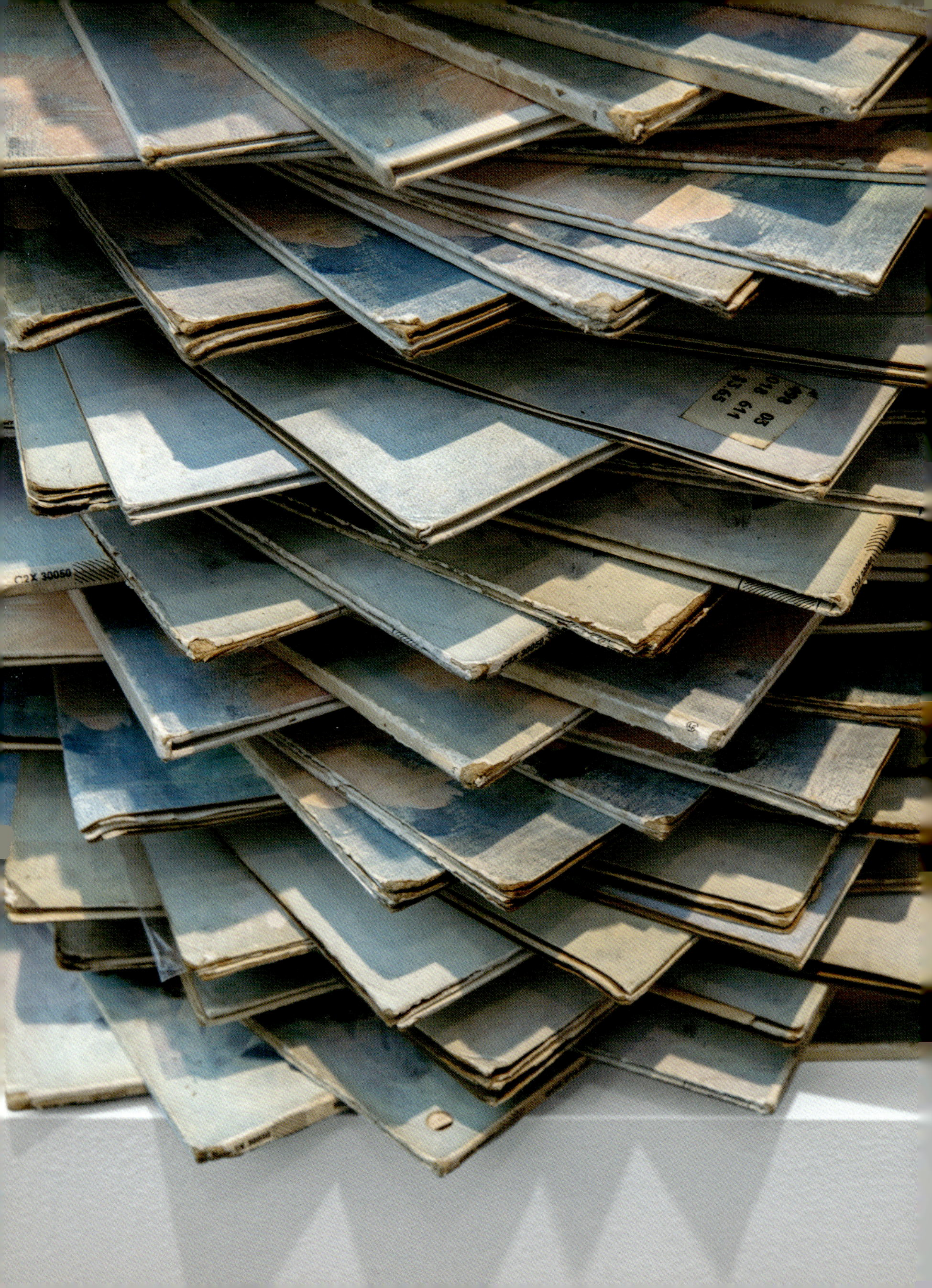
C2X 30050

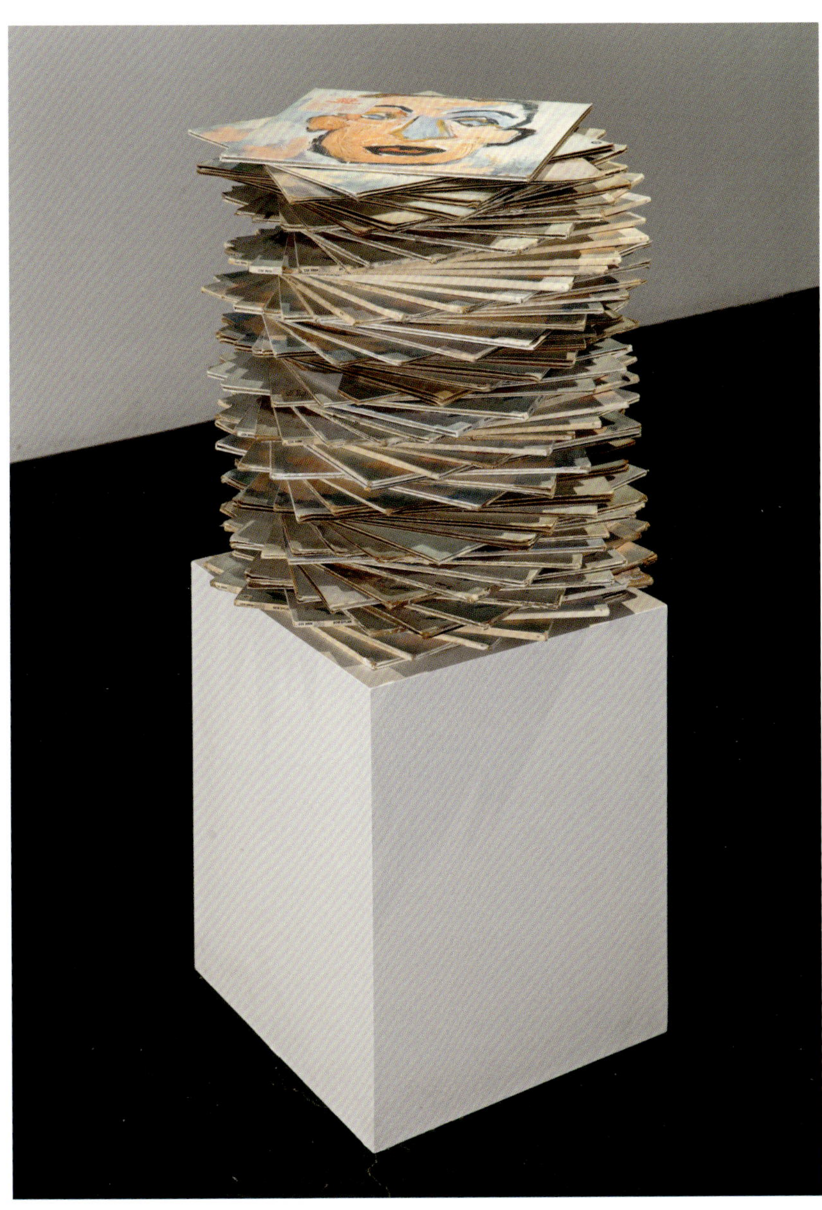

(above and detail facing)

Self Portrait,
2007–ongoing
Copies of Bob Dylan's
record *Self Portrait*
Dimensions variable

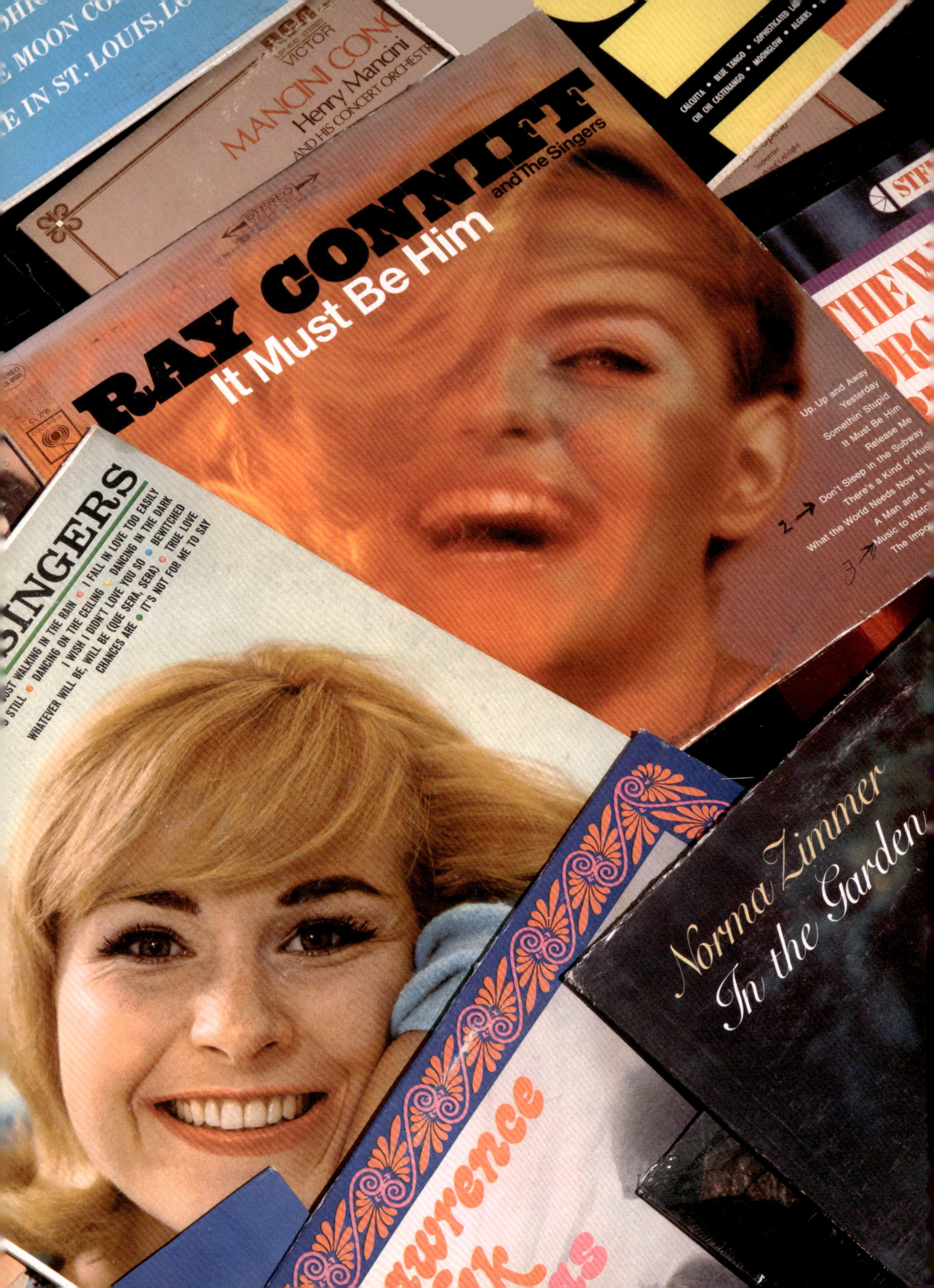

RCA VICTOR
Henry Mancini
AND HIS CONCERT ORCHESTRA
CALCUTTA • BLUE TANGO • SOPHISTICATED
CHI CHI CASTENANGO • MOONGLOW • ALGIERS
STEREO
RAY CONNIFF
and The Singers
It Must Be Him
Up, Up and Away
Yesterday
Somethin' Stupid
It Must Be Him
Release Me
Don't Sleep in the Subway
SINGERS
I FALL IN LOVE TOO EASILY
DANCING ON THE CEILING • DANCING IN THE DARK
I WISH I DIDN'T LOVE YOU SO • BEWITCHED
WHATEVER WILL BE, WILL BE (QUE SERA, SERA) • TRUE LOVE
CHANCES ARE • IT'S NOT FOR ME TO SAY
Norma Zimmer
In the Garden

CHECKLIST

All works courtesy of the artist; installation furniture by Ken Landauer/Fn Furniture

1
Curtain Call, 2018
Video
11 minutes

2
Uneasy Listening, 2018
Mixed media
Dimensions variable

3
Library of Ideas, 2018
Mixed media
Dimensions variable

4
Cartoons, 2018
16 archival inkjet prints
24 x 30 inches each

- *Art History*
- *Church of Thirst*
- *Coffin Full of Beans*
- *Google Cross Stitch*
- *Gray Crayons*
- *Hobo Supermen*
- *Ice Cream Flavors*
- *My Gravestone*
- *Naked Songwriting for Dummies*
- *Neolithic Fertility Ashtray*
- *Porno Classics*
- *Sad Balloons*
- *Self Esteem for Men*
- *Shack of Sit*
- *The Collector*
- *The First Solar-Powered Monet Poster*

5
Light Comedy Grave Rubbings, 2018
17 works, crayon on paper
Installation dimensions variable

- *A Purdy Outhouse*
- *Boner*
- *Burns Fumes*
- *COCKS*
- *Daniel Fish & Thankful Fish*
- *DIM*
- *Donald C Trump*
- *F'Real*
- *Giddy Family*
- *I was hoping for a pyramid*
- *Lily Zero*
- *Lotta Saviors Rising*
- *Mrs Patience Death*
- *Myron Cashdollar*
- *Seward / Optimist*
- *Snow White*
- *TAPE*

6
South Sea Selfies, 2017
Digital photographs, iPod, selfie stick
Dimensions variable

7
It's OK to Hate Yourself, 2015
Video
43 minutes

8
Counting In, 2015
Video
3 minutes, 30 seconds

9
VTV, 2011
Video
21 minutes

10
Tunisian Radios, 2008–2018
Video
12 minutes, 20 seconds

11
Self Portrait, 2007–ongoing
Copies of Bob Dylan's record *Self Portrait*
Dimensions variable

Uneasy Listening (detail), 2018
Mixed media
Dimensions variable

TIM DAVIS

BORN IN BLANTYRE, MALAWI IN 1969

LIVES AND WORKS IN NEW YORK

EDUCATION

2001
M.F.A., Yale University, New Haven, Connecticut

1991
B.A., Bard College, Annandale-on-Hudson, New York

SOLO EXHIBITIONS

2018
Opener 31: Tim Davis—When We Are Dancing (I Get Ideas), The Frances Young Tang Teaching Museum and Art Gallery, Skidmore College, Saratoga Springs, New York, October 20–January 6, 2019

2015
Elevator Music 29: Tim Davis: Unphotographable, The Frances Young Tang Teaching Museum and Art Gallery, Skidmore College, Saratoga Springs, New York, May 2–September 13

2014
Tim Davis: Forgeries, Van Doren Waxter, New York, September 10–October 31

2013
Quinto Quarto, Rome Commission 2013, Fotografia: Festival Internazionale di Roma, Museum of Contemporary Art of Rome, Rome, Italy, October 5–December 8

2012
Dollar General Drive By, Scotiabank Nuit Blanche, Toronto, Canada, September 29–30

The Upstate New York Olympics, Moscow Photobiennale, Moscow, Russia, March 30–May 9

2011
Tim Davis: The New Antiquity, Galleria Marabini, Bologna, Italy, September 29–November 11

Tim Davis: The Upstate New York Olympics, Smith College Museum of Art, Northampton, Massachusetts, June 17–August 28

The Upstate New York Olympics: Tim Davis, Samuel Dorsky Museum of Art at SUNY New Paltz, New Paltz, New York, March 30–July 17

2009
Tim Davis: Seeing Through History, DuBois Fort Visitor Center, New Paltz, New York, September 19–October 20

My Life in Politics, Ruffin Gallery, University of Virginia, Charlottesville, Virginia, September 25–October 23

The New Antiquity, Greenberg Van Doren Gallery, New York, September 10–October 24

2008
My Life in Politics, Luckman Fine Arts Complex, California State University, Los Angeles, California, November 1–December 20

Kings of Cyan, Mitterrand + Sanz, Zürich, Switzerland, August 30–October 18

2007
SubUrban: Permanent Collection, Knoxville Museum of Art, Knoxville, Tennessee, March 23–July 8

2006
Tim Davis: My Life in Politics, Museum of Contemporary Photography, Chicago, Illinois, August 18–October 14

Illilluminations, Greenberg Van Doren Gallery, New York, February 9–March 18

Permanent Collection, Susanne Vielmetter Los Angeles Projects, Los Angeles, California, January 21–February 18

2005
Tim Davis, Galerie Edward Mitterrand, Geneva, Switzerland, November 3–December 17

Permanent Collection, Kevin Bruk Gallery, Miami, Florida

Permanent Collection, Jackson Fine Art, Atlanta, Georgia, May 6–June 25

2004
My Life in Politics, Bohen Foundation, New York, September 11–November 5

Tim Davis, Rencontres d'Arles, Arles, France, July 8–September 19

2003
Permanent Collection, Brent Sikkema Gallery, New York

Tim Davis, Galerie Edward Mitterrand, Geneva, Switzerland, September 18–November 3

Tim Davis, Marella Arte Contemporanea, Milan, Italy, June 10–July 19

2002
Tim Davis, Galerie Rodolphe Janssen, Brussels, Belgium, October 17—November 30

2001
Retail, White Cube, London, England, April 25–May 26

Hypoluxo Road, Brent Sikkema Gallery, New York, November 27–December 22

SELECTED GROUP EXHIBITIONS

2019
Fotografi a Roma, Museo di Roma, Rome, Italy, April 17–September 22

Relazioni, L'Ospitale, Rubiera, Reggio Emilia, Italy, April 13–June 9

The Thingness of Things: Portraits of Objects, Allen Memorial Art Museum, Oberlin College, Oberlin, Ohio, February 5–July 14

2018
possible selves: queer foto vernaculars, Williams College Museum of Art, Williams College, Williamstown, Massachusetts, December 14–April 14, 2019

2017
Fotodocks 2017:Me:We, Städtische Kunsthalle München, Munich, Germany, September 23–October 23

Sonic Rebellion: Music as Resistance, Museum of Contemporary Art Detroit, Detroit, Michigan, September 8–January 7

2016
Festival Internazional di Roma, Piazza Vittorio Emanuele II, Rome, Italy, October 21–January 8

WIWTFDT, Joshua Liner Gallery, New York, October 13–November 12

It Takes a Nation: Art for Social Justice, American University Museum at the Katzen Arts Center, Washington, D.C., September 6–October 23

LUX: The Radiant Sea, Yancey Richardson Gallery, New York, July 14–August 19

The Rome Commission, Italian Cultural Institute, London, England, May 16–July 9

2015
Dear Dave, Week: Approaching 20 Issues in Print, Foley Gallery, New York, April 16–April 19

2014
Unknown: Pictures of Strangers, Transformer Station, Cleveland, Ohio, June 27–September 27

Postscript: Writing After Conceptual Art, Eli and Edythe Broad Art Museum at Michigan State University, East Lansing, Michigan, March 21–September 21

Small Works Exhibition, International Visions Gallery, Washington, D.C., February 6–March 15

Unsparing Quality, Diane Rosenstein Gallery, Los Angeles, California, February 1–March 29

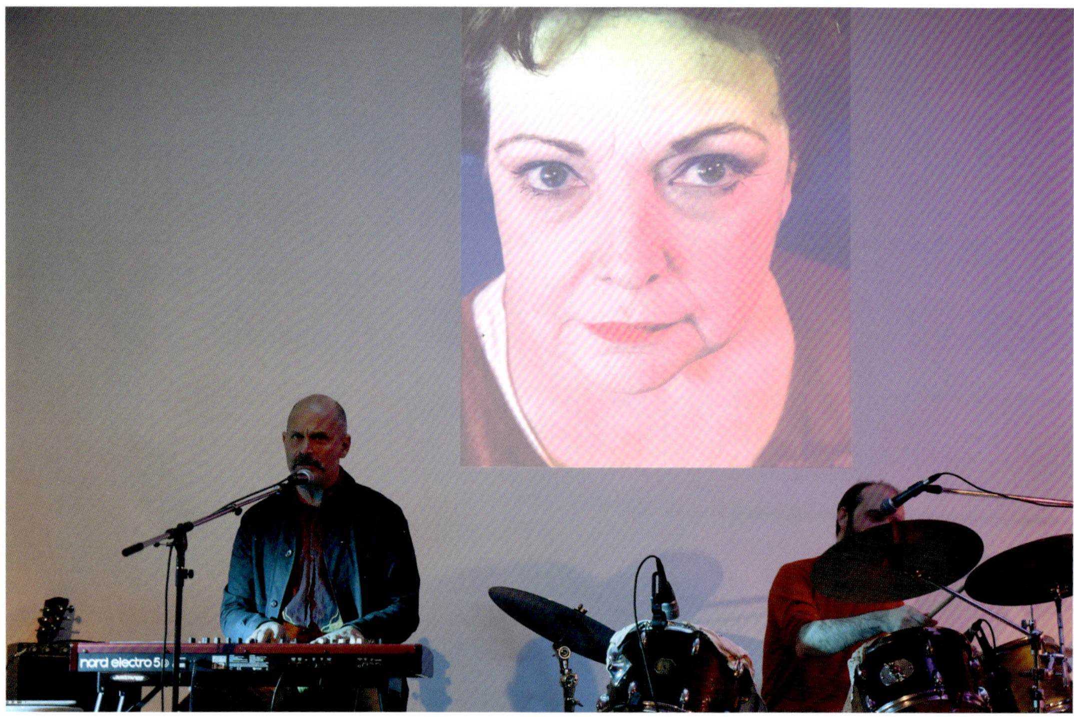

Severely Brothers (pictured: Tim Davis and Ben Fundis) performance view, Tang Museum, Saratoga Springs, New York, December 6, 2018

2012

Postscript: Writing After Conceptual Art, Museum of Contemporary Art, Denver, Colorado, October 12–February 3, 2013

Contemporary Russian Photography: Fotofest 2012 Biennial, Houston, Texas, March 16–April 29

34th Annual Photography Regional, Opalka Gallery, Albany, New York, March 15–April 21

Heavy Rotation, Franklin Street Works, Stamford, Connecticut, February 24–March 16

Spies in the House of Art: Photography, Film, and Video, Metropolitan Museum of Art, New York, February 7–August 26

2011

LOL, Albany International Airport Gallery, Albany, New York, October 1–March 25, 2012

Fotografia: Festival Internazionale di Roma, Museo d'Arte Contemporanea Roma, Rome, Italy, September 23–October 23

Biel/Bienne Festival of Photography, Biel/Bienne, Switzerland, September 2–25

The Life and Death of Buildings, Princeton University Art Museum, Princeton, New Jersey, July 23–November 6

Public Works, Museum of Contemporary Photography, Chicago, Illinois, April 29–July 17

Vassar 150 Years Later: New Photography by Tina Barney, Tim Davis, and Katherine Newbegin, The Frances Lehman Loeb Art Center, Vassar College, Poughkeepsie, New York, January 28–April 27

2010

B Sides: A Dialogue with Contemporary U.S. Photography, FotoFest, Inc., Houston, Texas, October 21–December 11

Lush Life, On Stellar Rays, New York, June 23–July 30

Town & Country, Tibor de Nagy Gallery, New York, June 17–August 11

Remains of Today, Brancolini Grimaldi, Rome, Italy, February 18–March 21

2009

Surface Tension: Contemporary Photographs from the Collection, The Metropolitan Museum of Art, New York, September 15–June 13, 2010

Two Years, Galerie Mitterrand & Sanz, Zurich, Switzerland, January 22–February 28

2008

The Innerworld of the Outerworld of the Innerworld, Von Lintel Gallery, New York, November 20–January 24, 2009

Sign/Age: Signs Signs Everywhere a Sign, Armand Bartos Fine Art, New York, September 26–October 24

To: Night (Contemporary Representations of the Night), Times Square Gallery, Hunter College, New York, September 25–November 15, and The Bertha and Karl Leubsdorf Art Gallery, Hunter College, New York, September 25–December 6

States of Mind: Young American Photography, CityScape, Brussels, Belgium, October 24–November 1

Fotografia: Festival Internazionale di Roma, VII Edition, Palazzo delle Esposizioni, Italy, April 4–May 25

Beware of the Wolf, American Academy in Rome, Rome, Italy, March 20–April 2

Vernissage Jeudi, Galerie Mitterrand & Sanz, Zürich, Switzerland, March 6–April 12

The Leisure Suite, The LeRoy Neiman Gallery, Columbia University, New York, January 24–February 14

2007

New Photography from the KMA Collection, Knoxville Museum of Art, Knoxville, Tennessee, October 12–March 16, 2008

The Irresistible Force, Tate Modern, London, England, September 20–November 25

View Thirteen: Practical f/x, Mary Boone Gallery, New York, September 6–October 27

Midsummer's Eve: Emerging International Photographers, Aftermodern Gallery, San Francisco, California

Easy Rider: Road Trips Through America, Yancey Richardson Gallery, New York, July 11–September 8

Site Inscription, Paul Rodgers/9W Gallery, New York, June 7–July 21

Prints, Nelson Hancock Gallery, New York

Outpost, Susanne Hilberry Gallery, Ferndale, Michigan, March 23–April 28

2006

The Gold Standard, MoMA P.S.1, Queens, New York, October 29–January 15, 2007

The Office: In and Out of the Box, Dorsky Gallery, Long Island City, New York, September 10–November 13

Tim Davis et Virginie Morillo, Mitterrand + Cramer, Geneva, Switzerland, September 14–November 4

Taken For Looks, Southeast Museum of Photography, Daytona Beach, Florida, May 24–September 1

2005

The New City: Sub/urbia in Recent Photography, The Whitney Museum of American Art, New York, September 30–January 15, 2006

Introductions, Greenberg Van Doren Gallery, New York, July 14–September 30

2005 Leopold Godowsky, Jr. Color Photography Awards, Photographic Resource Center at Boston University, Boston, Massachusetts, July 8–August 7

On View: Photographing the Museum, Yancey Richardson Gallery, New York, July 8–September 17

Slow Down, Pilar Parra & Romero Galeria de Arte, Madrid, Spain, June 19–July 17

Tête à Tête, Greenberg Van Doren Gallery, New York, June 8–July 8

Life and Limb, Feigen Contemporary, New York, June 3–July 30

This Must Be The Place, Center for Curatorial Studies, Bard College, Annandale-on-Hudson, New York, February 6–20

Still Life and Stilled Lives, Ariel Meyerowitz Gallery, New York, January 28–March 19

Second Sight: Originality, Duplicity and the Object, The Frances Lehman Loeb Art Center, Vassar College, Poughkeepsie, New York, January 14–April 10

2004
Architecture and Arts 1900–2000, Genova Palazzo Ducale, Genoa, Italy, October 2–February 13, 2005

2003
The Office, The Photographers Gallery, London, England, November 27–January 18, 2004

Jessica Stockholder, Gorney, Bravin & Lee, New York, October 10–November 15

Super You, Daniel Silverstein Gallery, New York, June 5–July 1

2002
American Standard: (Para) Normality and Everyday Life, Barbara Gladstone Gallery, New York, June 26–August 16

The Dubrow Biennial, Kagan Martos Gallery, New York

2001
Boomerang: Collectors Choice, Exit Art, New York

Summer 2001, Brent Sikkema Gallery, New York

Size Matters, Edwynn Houk Gallery, New York

Settings & Players: Theatrical Ambiguity in American Photography, White Cube, London, March 9–April 14

Workspheres, Museum of Modern Art, New York, February 8–April 22

AMERICAN, Postmasters Gallery, New York, January 6–February 10

2000
Foreign Bodies: Art, Medicine, Technology, Untitled(space), New Haven, Connecticut

New York Now 2000: Contemporary Work in Photography, Museum of the City of New York

Representing the Intangible, Photographic Resource Center, Boston, Massachusetts, March 10–April 28

Thinner Air: Minimalism in Photography, Society for Contemporary Photography, Kansas City, Missouri

1999
Thin Air: A Group Show of Minimalist Photographs, Julie Saul Gallery, New York, July 8–August 20

1998
Photo (Op), Geoffrey Young Gallery, Great Barrington, Massachusetts

BIBLIOGRAPHY

SELECTED BOOKS AND CATALOGUES

American Standard. Exhibition catalogue. New York: Barbara Gladstone Gallery, 2002.

America: Three Hundred Years of Innovation. Exhibition catalogue. Shanghai, China: Shanghai Museum of Art, 2007.

Davis, Tim and Jack Hitt. *My Life in Politics*. Reading, Pennsylvania: Aperture/ Blindspot, 2006.

Davis, Tim and Marco Delogu. *Quinto Quarto*. Exhibition catalogue. Rome, Italy: Punctum Press, 2013.

Davis, Tim. *Permanent Collection*. Paso Robles, California: Nazraeli Press, 2005.

———. *American Whatever*. Washington, D.C.: Edge Books, 2004.

———. *Lots*. Paris, France: Coromandel Design, 2002.

———. *Dailies*. Great Barrington, Massachusetts: The Figures Press, 2000.

Demos, T.J. *Vitamin Ph: New Perspectives in Photography*. London: Phaidon Press, 2006.

Fabry, Alexis, Céline Fribourg, and Grégory Leroy. *Séduire/ Seduce*. Exhibition catalogue. Paris, France: Coromandel Express, 2002.

Guerrieri, William and Tiziana Serena. *Il Tecnogiro Dell' Ornitorinco*. Bologne, Italy: Damiani, 2010.

Neri, Louise. *Settings & Players, Theatrical Ambiguity in American Photography*. Exhibition catalogue. London, England: *White Cube2*, 2001.

Pierre, Frédéric and Camille Françoise. *Tell Mum Everything is OK #3 – 'A Postmodern World.'* Artist's book. Nantes, France: Editions FP&CF, 2010.

Prose, Francine and Tim Davis. *Tim Davis: The New Antiquity*. Exhibition catalogue. Bologna, Italy: Galleria Marabini, 2010.

Self, Dana. *Tim Davis Permanent Collection*. Exhibition catalogue. Knoxville, Tennessee: Knoxville Museum of Art, 2007.

Seligman, Rachel, ed. *Opener 31: Tim Davis — When We Are Dancing (I Get Ideas)*. Exhibition catalogue. Saratoga Springs, New York: The Frances Young Tang Teaching Museum and Art Gallery at Skidmore College, 2020.

Wallace, Brian and Tim Davis. *The Upstate New York Olympics*. Exhibition catalogue. New Paltz, New York: Samuel Dorsky Museum of Art, 2011.

SELECTED ARTICLES AND REVIEWS

Ahlander, Astri von Arbin. "Tim Davis." *The Days of Yore*, January 10, 2011.

Aletti, Vince. "Tim Davis, Shortlist: Photo." *The Village Voice*, December 11, 2001.

———. "Tim Davis." *The Village Voice*, September 19, 2003.

———. "Tim Davis: My Life in Politics." *The Village Voice*, November 1, 2004.

———. "Too Blessed to be Depressed." *Modern Painters* (May 2006): 48.

Alexander, Lorraine. "Vassar on View." *The Millbrook Independent*, February 16, 2011.

"Coming Back in Style." *Art + Auction* (September 2005): 116–118.

Dimopoulos, Thomas. "Artist Returns to Spa City for Major Art Show at Tang." *Saratoga Today*, October 19, 2018.

Douglas, Sarah. "Tim Davis: My Life in Politics." *Artnet*, September 27, 2004.

Dunham, Carla Ruth. "Tim Davis." *ArtUS*, iss. 13 (May–June 2006): 46.

Dykstra, Jean. "Tim Davis: Greenberg Van Doren." *Art in America* 97, iss. 11 (December 2009): 135–136.

———. "Dispatches From the Brink." *Art in America* 98, iss. 6 (June/July 2010): 77–80.

"Easy Rider." *New Yorker*, August 20, 2007.

"Eye." *V Magazine*, (January–February 2002).

Gabler, Jay. "Critic's Picks: The Sports Show, the Minneapolis Institute of Art." *Artforum* (April 2012).

Griffin, Amy. "LOL: Airport Gallery has fun with humor." *Times Union*, December 5, 2011.

"Introductions." *New Yorker*, September 19, 2005.

Johnson, Ken. "'Introductions.'" *New York Times*, August 15, 2005.

Jentleson, Katherine. "Madrid: Raging Bull." *Art + Auction* (February 2007): 39.

Kimmelman, Michael. "Tim Davis: My Life in Politics." *New York Times*, October 8, 2004.

Klaasmeyer, Kelly. "The Best 'B-Sides'." *Houston Press*, December 1, 2010.

Laster, Paul. "Tim Davis, 'The New Antiquity.'" *Time Out New York*, September 23, 2009.

Lauf, Cornelia. "Beware of the Wolf." *Art in America* 96, iss. 9 (October 2008): 202.

McLaren, Duncan. "Tim Davis, White Cube, London." *The Independent*, May 13, 2001.

Nichols, Matthew Guy. "Tim Davis at Brent Sikkema." *Art in America* 91, iss. 11 (November 2003): 160–161.

Pavia, Jessica. "Down the Rabbit Hole and Into Tim Davis' Mind." *Skidmore News*, October 17, 2018.

Pollack, Barbara. "Tim Davis at Brent Sikkema." *Art in America* (June 2002).

———. "Tim Davis, 'Illuminations.'" *Time Out New* York, March 16, 2006.

Pulimood, Steve. "Interview with Tim Davis." *Whitehot Magazine* (April 2008).

Rosenberg, Karen. "Show and Tell: Tim Davis." *New York Magazine*, February 13, 2006.

———. "Into the Darkroom, With Pulleys, Jam and Snakes." *New York Times*, November 6, 2009.

Schwendener, Martha. "Tim Davis: My Life in Politics." *Artforum* (January 2005).

Shmerler, Sarah. "New York Gallery Beat." *Art on Paper* (March–April 2002).

Slade, George. "Review: My Life in Politics." *Photo-Eye Booklist* 28, iss. 2 (Summer 2006): 15–17.

Smith, Roberta. "Tim Davis at Brent Sikkema Gallery." *New York Times*, December 14, 2001.

"Still Life & Stilled Lives." *ARTnews* (October 2005): 170.

Stillman, Nick. "Life and Limb." *Time Out New York*, July 21–27, 2005.

"Tim Davis." *Draft* (Spring 2006): 25-35.

"Tim Davis: Illuminations." *Eleven Eleven (1111) Journal of Literature and Art III* (2006): 20.

"Tim Davis: My Life in Politics." *Positive (Pozytyw)*, iss. 7 (2005): 72–80.

"Tim Davis." *New Yorker*, December 17 and 24, 2001.

Uneasy Listening, 2018
Mixed media
Dimensions variable
Installation view, Tang Museum, Saratoga Springs, New York, 2018

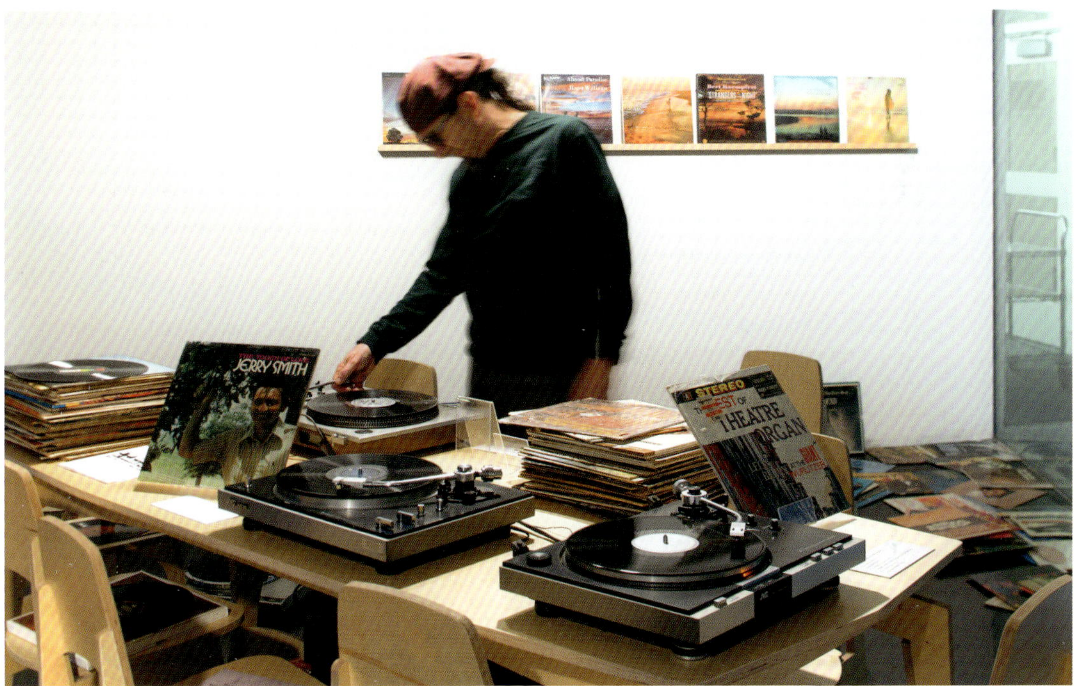

"Tim Davis." *New Yorker*, September 22, 2003.

"Tim Davis." *New Yorker*, October 11, 2004.

"Tim Davis." *New Yorker*, March 20, 2006.

"Tim Davis." *New Yorker*, October 5, 2009.

"Tim Davis." *The Village* Voice, March 8, 2006.

"Tim Davis." *Time Out New York*, December 13–27, 2001.

Tysh, George. "Three degrees of saturation: Susanne Hillberry offers up a trio of unsettling photographers." *Metrotimes*, April 4, 2007.

"Wild Kingdom." *Time Out New York*, February 9, 2006.

Wolff, Rachel. "Tim Davis: Greenberg Van Doren." *ARTnews* (November 2009): 118–119.

Woodward, Richard B. "Altered States." *Artnews* (March 2006): 104.

Zollner, Manfred. "Abschied von der Komfortzone / Farewell to the Comfort Zone." *European Photography* 31, iss. 87 (Summer 2010): 5–7.

ACKNOWLEDGMENTS

TIM DAVIS — WHEN WE ARE DANCING (I GET IDEAS) presents recent work by an artist whose combination of versatility, curiosity, empathy and humor is unparalleled. I am deeply indebted to him for his collaborative enthusiasm, joie de vivre, and general amazingness as we made this exhibition together. It has been one of the great pleasures of my curatorial career.

Special thanks to writer and critic Luc Sante for writing a new piece for this catalogue as well as his participation in the You Are a Collector storytelling event. Many thanks to all those who participated in the wonderful programs that were presented at the Tang Museum in conjunction with the exhibition, including The Severely Brothers (Tim Davis, vocals, keyboard, and guitar; Dan D'Oca, lead guitar; Ben Fundis, drums and vocals; John Rosenthal, bass; and Kim Seeger, rhythm guitar and vocals); Janet Borgerson and Jonathan Schroeder who participated in the Hi-Fi Living and Uneasy Listening Brown Bag Lunch and Conversation, and the participants of the You Are a Collector storytelling event: Erica Wojcik, Psychology Department, Skidmore College; George DeMers, Short Order Cook, Skidmore College; John Anzalone, World Languages Department, Skidmore College; Sam Vogel '19, Skidmore College student; Hadia Bakkar '20, Skidmore College student; Brittany Watts-Hendrixs '20, Skidmore College Student; Mimi Lipson, writer, author of the story collection *The Cloud of Unknowing*; and Kevin Factor, host of the podcast "Foraging Ahead."

Many thanks to Ken Landauer of Fn Furniture for working with us to make the elegant furniture featured in the exhibition; it was integral to the installations of both the *Library of Ideas* and *Uneasy Listening*.

Thanks also to curatorial assistant Molly Channon for her careful attention to all aspects of this project, and to student Exhibitions Assistants Dayna Joseph '19, E.B. Sciales '19, and Jane Cole '21, for their hard work compiling and editing content for this catalogue. The entire staff of the Tang Museum contributed to this project and I would like to thank them all: Ian Berry, Isolde Brielmaier, Jeanne Eddy, Jean Tschanz-Egger, Sophie Heath, Michael Janairo, Elizabeth Karp, Annelise Kelly, Jessica Lubniewski, Neal Matherne, Rebecca McNamara, Sunny Ra, Patti Sopp, kelly ward, Nick Warner, Tom Yoshikami, and Cynthia Zellner. Thanks also to the installation crew, Sarah Bates, Brandon Bissel-Evans, Patrick Casey, Pat Girard, and Mike Millspaugh. And many thanks to our designer Beverly Joel, and to photographers Arthur Evans, Jeremy Lawson, and Modern Mix.

— Rachel Seligman, Assistant Director for Curatorial Affairs
and Malloy Curator

IN EVERY ARTIST'S DREAMS THERE ARE INSTITUTIONS who answer each inquiry with "yes." Those who get to work with staff of the Tang Museum get to see that dream come true. Making *When We Are Dancing (I Get Ideas)* come true was a long, complex, engaged, collaborative process, and everyone at the Tang handled each step with resilience, kindness, flexibility and aplomb. Rachel Seligman drove this runaway sledge across the tundra to completion and I've never worked with a curator as empowering as she. Often making a show feels like trying to carry a couch up a flight of stairs: twisting, turning upside down, backing down into a corner. Every time it felt that way, Rachel pointed to a crack in the corridor and an elevator mysteriously opened peopled with smiling handypeople. I had never done a show of this scale and ambition, with this many moving parts and the guidance and surety of the entire staff should've been up there on the marquee with me. I'd like to thank Ian Berry, Molly Channon, Michael Janairo, Elizabeth Karp, Annelise Kelly, Sunny Ra, Jean Tschanz-Egger, Tom Yoshikami, kelly ward, Patti Sopp, Rebecca McNamara, and Cynthia Zellner for all their support, and Frank Moscowitz and Nick Warner for their sonic and technical expertise.

This show absorbed ten years of projects and its enablers are legion. First: Lisa Sanditz, without whom none of this would have been possible. She is my greatest interlocutor, first to see, edit, alter and encourage . . . my favorite human. Ken Landauer and Julianne Swartz deserve special mention, first as artists who have always loved my work and helped me shepherd me around discouragement, second as friends, third as inspirations, and lastly, in the case of Ken's *FN Furniture*, as collaborator on the design of the show. Stephen Shore and my colleagues at Bard College Photography Program have provided such an extraordinarily rich and productive work environment over these last, gulp, fifteen years, enabling all this work to be made while teaching and making my photographic projects. Also, the Bard Research Fund paid for the production of *It's OK To Hate Yourself*.

I'd like to thank all the bands who unwittingly participated in *Counting In*, and to acknowledge Dorsey Waxter and Liz Sadeghi for encouraging its screening at various art fairs. Joe Hagan was orchestral in our many discussions about Easy Listening music during our regular LP listening sessions *chez lui*. Thanks to those of you who helped with *Light Comedy Grave Rubbings*: Bix Davis, Birdie and Enna Rae Sherwin, Helaine Selin and Bob Rakoff, Conrad Bakker of Untitled Projects, Eleanor Rust, Tom Hoying, and Kristi Gibson.

Thanks to the students of Skidmore College for asking the tough questions.

— Tim Davis

This catalogue accompanies the exhibition

OPENER 31

TIM DAVIS: WHEN WE ARE DANCING (I GET IDEAS)

The Frances Young Tang Teaching Museum and Art Gallery at Skidmore College
Saratoga Springs, New York
October 20, 2018–January 6, 2019

The Frances Young Tang Teaching Museum and Art Gallery at Skidmore College
815 North Broadway
Saratoga Springs, NY 12866
T 518 580 8080
F 518 580 5069
www.tang.skidmore.edu

State of the Arts

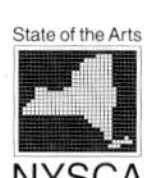

NYSCA

This exhibition and publication are made possible in part with public funds from the New York State Council on the Arts, a state agency, Ann Schapps Schaffer '62 and Mel Schaffer, Beverly Beatson Grossman '58, and the Friends of the Tang.

ISBN: 978-0-9982422-3-1

Library of Congress Control Number: 2019951396

Pages: 10, 34–35, 38–39, 46, 50–67, 85–86: Arthur Evans
Pages 17, 80: Modern Mix
Pages 20, 75: Jeremy Lawson

Designed by Beverly Joel, pulp, ink.

Printed in Italy by Conti Tipocolor

Front cover:
Spiral Jetty Comb Over from *Cartoons*, 2018, 24 x 30 inches

Back cover:
Curtain Calls, 2018 [video still], video, 11 minutes

Page 1:
Library of Ideas (detail), 2018, mixed media, dimensions variable; pictured: *(When We Are Dancing) I Get Ideas*, music by Julio Sanders, lyrics by Dorcas Cochran, Los Angeles, California: Hill and Range Songs, Inc., 1951

Pages 2–3:
Hobo Supermen from *Cartoons*, 2018, archival inkjet print, 24 x 30 inches